Merry Christmas 1975

Bishop McGuinness
Memorial High School

North Carolina

COLONIAL

North Carolina

by
Eugenia Burney

THOMAS NELSON INC., PUBLISHERS

Nashville   New York

Photographs courtesy of the North Carolina Museum of History. Permission is gratefully acknowledged.

First edition

Library of Congress Cataloging in Publication Data

Burney, Eugenia.
  Colonial North Carolina.

6003

  (Colonial history series)
  Bibliography: p.
  SUMMARY: Traces the history of North Carolina from its earliest settlement by Walter Raleigh to its becoming the twelfth state of the union in 1789.
    1. North Carolina—History—Colonial period, ca. 1600–1775—Juvenile literature. [1. North Carolina—History—Colonial period, ca. 1600–1775] I. Title.
F257.B88   975.6′02   75–20192
ISBN 0–8407–7134–7

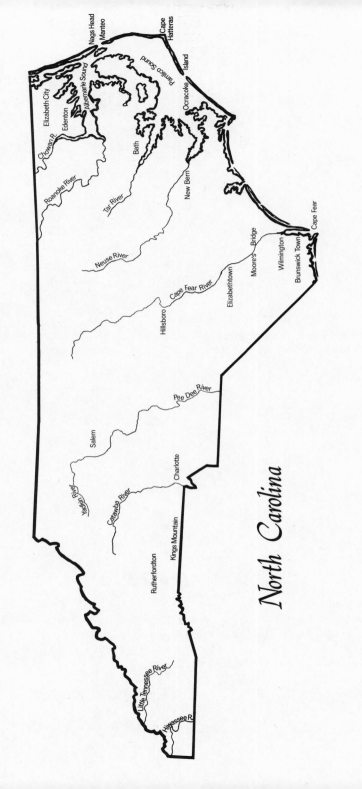

North Carolina

Contents

Devon-born Sir Walter Raleigh never saw the New World, but he lavished his own money on three voyages to North America. The Raleigh-backed colonies on Roanoke Island were the first settlements in what is now North Carolina.

CHAPTER ONE

The Relief Expedition

It was so dark that the landing party overshot its first mark. Then, seeing to the northward "the light of a great fire through the woods," they rowed for that instead. Surely fire meant human habitation, and a settlement of people is what they had come to this island to find.

But when the party—nineteen Englishmen in two boats—anchored just offshore of the fire, they saw no one. It was full night by then; perhaps the settlers were sleeping. The leader ordered one of his men to sound a trumpet, the traditional summons to announce that they had come openly in peace. There was no response to the call. The trumpeter then played a familiar English tune, and another and another. The men in the boats called out in friendly fashion, urging the people on land to come forth. But the only sound was the lapping of waves against the two hulls.

The place was Roanoke Island, the time the night of August 16–17, 1590. The nineteen Englishmen were led by John White, artist, gentleman, and governor of the "Cittie of Ralegh in Virginea." They had come to bring supplies and encouragement to a party of English colonists they had settled here three years before.

No member of the party had more stake in finding the settlement than Governor White himself. He was its official head, of course, but more importantly, he had left behind among the settlers his daughter Ellinor and her husband, Ananias Dare. Just before White had sailed for home, Ellinor had given birth to a daughter, the first child of English blood born in the New World. The Dares had named her for the colony they had hoped to start: Virginia. The day after tomorrow, August 18, would be her third birthday.

The landing party could do nothing more until morning, so the men settled down on the thwarts to doze away the hours of darkness. Finally, at dawn, they moved cautiously ashore.

A handsome scene greeted them—low sandy shore, "so full of grapes," wrote an earlier observer of a similar strand, "as the very beating and surge of the sea overflowed them." Beyond the sand lay grassland and scrub forest of cypress, cedar, and pine.

Here the party found "the grass and sundry rotten trees burning about the place," explaining the fire they had seen, but no evidence of settlement. They advanced through the woods a ways. Seeing nothing, they returned to their boats and continued along the shore of the island to their original destination—the site of Fort Raleigh, where the settlers had been left in 1587.

As they walked up the beach, familiar to John White from his previous visit, they saw the prints of bare feet "of two or three sorts," a sign that Indians had visited the settlement. Then, at the top of the sand bank, they stopped. A tree stood there with three letters carved on it: "CRO."

At the time Governor White left his colony to seek help for it, the settlers had been considering a move from Roanoke Island to some spot on the mainland. In case the decision was to relocate, White had arranged with them a "secret token" to let him know where they had gone. They were to carve on a tree or doorpost the name of their destination, and if they had left Roanoke in distress, they were to mark a Christian cross above the letters.

"CRO," the landing party reasoned, must stand for "Croatoan," the name of an island nearby and of a friendly tribe of Indians who lived there. There was no cross above the letters. And the pinnace, the small sailing vessel that had been left with them, was missing.

So far, so good. As they moved up toward the settlers' village and fort, they found a prominent tree—by tradition, a live oak—where "in fair capital letters" the full word was carved: "CROATOAN." It too had no cross above it.

But when the Englishmen looked around them, they were not altogether reassured. The rude dwelling huts of the settlers had been torn down to make room for an enlargement of the fort, which had been greatly strengthened with a palisade of "great trees" and bastions at the corners. Why should colonists invest effort in rebuilding their fort if they were planning to move peacefully away?

Inside the palisade, there was evidence of the place having been ransacked by ignorant hands. Bars of iron and lead lay scattered about, as did fowling pieces and cannonballs. Chests, some of which White recognized as his, had been broken open and the contents scattered: "My books torn from their covers, pictures and maps rotten from the rain, and my armour almost eaten through with rust."

Still, the word "CROATOAN" seemed to imply that all might yet be well. The party had only to row back to their ships, now anchored in deep water about ten miles away, and sail to Croatoan. If the English settlers were no longer there, the friendly Indians would surely know where they had gone.

But it wasn't so simple as that. There were navigation and weather problems.

The coast along which the English were scouting was one of the most dangerous in the world—a flat, sandy mainland, bordered by a series of broad, shallow bodies of water called sounds, shielded in turn from the open ocean by a chain of low sandbars. In these shoal waters, large ships could not anchor close in. Even small rowing boats sometimes foundered in attempting to pass into the sounds, for wind and sea constantly shifted the treacherous sands, and the passages through them, called inlets, opened and closed as the elements chose. On this very voyage, one of John White's boats had capsized while crossing the bar, killing six sailors. As if geography weren't bad enough, the weather in this region was—and is—notoriously foul. This chain of low sandbars is today known officially as the Outer Banks, unofficially as the Graveyard of the Atlantic.

As John White's landing party reboarded the ships and prepared to sail for Croatoan, a storm came up and three anchors were lost—bad news for a sailing vessel even under balmy skies. With the hurricane season at hand, the vessels' masters were afraid to linger off the Banks any longer. The colony had waited three years for help, they reasoned; one year more couldn't make much difference. The expedition to Croatoan was postponed, and the ships sailed for home.

Governor John White and his followers could not have known it, of course, but they had just taken part in one of the best known and most graphic incidents in American history. And they were among the first groups of white men to set foot in what would later come to be known as North Carolina.

CHAPTER TWO

Sir Walter Raleigh

J ohn White's colony was not the first English attempt to settle the New World, or even the first settlement on Roanoke Island. But like most expeditions that had set foot on this region before, it had its origins in the brain of one of the most remarkable men of the sixteenth century: Sir Walter Raleigh.

Born in 1552 in the seafaring county of Devon—home also of Drake and Hawkins—Walter Raleigh, or Ralegh, had grown up in the great age of exploration and discovery. In his youth he must have heard and read many tales of great voyages. In 1492, Christopher Columbus, a Genoese sailing for Spain, discovered a vast landmass lying between Europe and Asia, and proved that the world was round. Five years later, John Cabot, another Genoese, carried the banner of the English king to the region of Newfoundland (and gave England the basis for her later claim to colonize the entire northern colony). In 1513 Juan Ponce de Léon, in 1519 Hernando Cortes, in 1531 Francisco Pizarro, in 1539 Hernando de Soto, in 1540 Francisco de Coronado—and many others at other times—explored the Americas for the honor of Spain.

Raleigh might also have read of the voyages of Giovanni da Verrazano, a gentlemanly Florentine navigator who sailed for Francis I of France. In command of the first French expedition to cross the Atlantic, he sailed his ship *Dauphine* to look for a passage to China. In March, 1524, Verrazano concluded that he had reached a part of the American coast that had not been discovered by the earlier explorers. At the mouth of what is now the Cape Fear River, south of modern Wilmington, North Carolina, he wrote in his report to King Francis:

"We discouered a new land, neuer before seene of any man either ancient or moderne. . . . We preceiued by the great fires that we saw by the Sea coast, that it was inhabited."

As the *Dauphine* continued to sail up the coast, the natives came to the beach and indicated by friendly signs that the white men would be welcome ashore. One young sailor dived into the water carrying some little bells, mirrors, and other small gifts for the Indians. He swam near the shore, threw the presents to the natives, and began to swim back toward the ship, but the heavy surf washed him ashore. When the Indians saw him on the beach, they "ran and took him up by the head, legs and arms, and carried him to a distance from the surf." The captive shrieked in fear, but the Indians were only trying to warm and revive the young man, and soon saw him back to the boat.

Thus began the first contact between the Indians of North Carolina and the first white men to see them.

In 1568, Raleigh entered Oriel College, Oxford, but he dropped out the next year to fight for the Huguenot cause in France. Then in 1578, his half-brother, Sir Humphrey Gilbert, who had long advocated an expedition in search of a "northwest passage" to India, was granted a patent to "discover and occupy remote heathen lands not actually possessed of any Christian prince or people." Sir Humphrey took young Walter with him.

The expedition did little exploring but much pirating among the Spaniards, and it returned home without reaching North America. Raleigh was then sent to Cork to help subdue some Irish rebels, and in December, 1581, he returned to England. Ambitious for advancement, he turned himself into one of Queen Elizabeth's courtiers.

He was now nearly thirty years old, at the peak of his manly beauty—a tall lithe body, dark hair, and suntanned skin set off by splendid dress and expensive jewels. He could fence, ride, and hunt with the best of them, and his quick wit brought laughter from his friends by directing barbed verses at his enemies. At the same time Raleigh was proud, haughty, and impatient with anything that did not suit him, lashing out bitterly at any subordinate who was slow or incompetent.

The well-known story of Raleigh throwing his beautiful cape over a muddy puddle of water in front of the queen may or may not be true. But the self-assured young man found some way to bring himself to Elizabeth's attention. She liked his ready wit and made him a favorite for a while. She knighted him and made him wealthy. He was able to get a second patent for his half-brother, Sir Humphrey Gilbert, although this time he remained at court when Gilbert sailed. On the way home, Sir Humphrey's ship was lost at sea, and the patent was left to Walter.

Raleigh saw his chance to attain an old ambition. With his new wealth and power, he would finance the first English colony in America.

Roanoke Island and the Outer Banks, as depicted by John White. North lies to the right. "Secotan" is modern Dare County, "Weapemeoc" represents modern Currituck County. The artist has shown wrecked ships along the treacherous coast, large vessels anchored in deep water offshore, a shallow-draft pinnace exploring Croatoan Sound.

Search for a Colony Site

Losing no time, Raleigh outfitted two small ships whose names have not been recorded. The flagship was commanded by a navigator named Philip Amadas, the consort by Arthur Barlowe. Raleigh directed them to explore the coast between the parallels of latitude 32 and 38 degrees north (in modern geographical terms, between Savannah, Georgia, and the southern boundary of Maryland). In order to avoid Spanish spies, the two little ships slipped secretly out of Plymouth on April 27, 1584.

On July 4 they sighted land, probably between present Cape Fear and Cape Lookout, a promontory at the southern end of the Outer Banks. Beyond the sandbar they could see an "inclosed sea," but even in their small vessels they could not find an inlet deep enough to enter.

At last, after sailing for 120 miles, they spied an inlet that seemed adequate. They sailed into it on July 13 and landed on Hatarask Island, one of the sandbars of the Banks. They were delighted with the abundance of grapes and trees, the many birds. Three days later they saw the first local Indians. Three men approached in a dugout canoe and landed near the ships' anchorage. One of the Indians was a werowance or subchief, and he told them that the country roundabout was called Windgandcon and was ruled by a head chief or king called Wingina. He was invited aboard one of the English ships and given a shirt and hat. In return, he and the other two Indians caught fish for the white men. The next day these three Indians returned with forty or fifty others to marvel at these strange newcomers.

Barlowe declared formal possession of the whole country "in the right of the Queen's most excellent majesty." He made a small column with the English arms rudely carved on it and waved the English flag over it as the wondering natives watched. It seemed to him that he had found an excellent region for Sir Walter's new colony.

The Englishmen spent several weeks exploring Roanoke Island as well as Pamlico and Albemarle sounds. Barlowe took a good look at the Indians and their habits and reported on them in some detail. "Their boates are made of one tree . . ." he wrote in his report. Their only edged tools were "out of a wrake . . . of some Christian ship . . . out of whose sides they drew the nayles and the spikes. . . ."

Two of these natives were so taken with the Englishmen and their marvelous belongings—timepieces, guns, burning glasses, bells—that they agreed to return with them to their homeland. Later, the two Indians, Manteo and Wanchese, were to be of some importance to English settlers of this region, for good and ill. Appropriately, their names are commemorated to this day in two towns on Roanoke Island.

On August 23, 1584, the expedition sailed for home. They landed in England about September 15.

Planning an Expedition

Sir Walter Raleigh had not been idle in England while Barlowe and Amadas were in America. He contacted Richard Hakluyt, the famed geographer and compiler of exploration narratives, and requested that he write *A Discourse Concerning Westerne Planting*, which the eager Hakluyt was only too glad to do. In the essay, Hakluyt urged the government to encourage colonization for two principal reasons: It would relieve the nation of such expendable persons as debtors, discharged soldiers, beggars' children, "valient youths rusting and hurtful by lack of employment," and nuisancy Puritan clergymen. And settlement being in a warmish climate, the colony could supply the mother country such Mediterranean products as wine and raisins, sugar, olives, citrus fruits, and dyestuffs.

Raleigh, adding Barlowe's narrative to Hakluyt's *Discourse*, hoped to induce the queen to subsidize his next venture.

Elizabeth was distracted by her troubles with Spain just then—news of the Invincible Armada, then abuilding, had reached England—but she did accept his suggestion that the Indian name Windgandcon be changed to Virginia. Whether this was in honor of the Virgin Queen or the virgin land, or both, is still in dispute. Even without her backing, Raleigh set about planning his new colony.

Apparently it never occurred to Sir Walter that farmers and carpenters would be needed to build a colony. His idea was that soldiers could erect a fort and live off the Indians until more colonists could be sent out as farmers. So he chose a scruffy lot of 108 men, mostly freebooters looking for easy money. But other members of the expedition were more distinguished.

Since the queen was still refusing to let Sir Walter leave the country, Raleigh named his cousin, hot-tempered but capable Sir Richard Grenville, commander-in-chief of the expedition. As the colony's governor, Sir Walter chose one Ralph Lane, a wealthy young gentleman of haughty disposition but with some important connections at court.

Believing that a scientist should accompany the expedition, Raleigh invited Thomas Hariot to come along. A slender man with a long face and thin neck, Hariot was an Oxford graduate and one of the finest mathematicians in England. His duties on the expedition included writing a report on the natural history of the region to be settled and drawing maps. When Manteo and Wanchese arrived in England, Hariot taught them English and tried to learn a little of the Algonkian language from them.

Manteo and Wanchese returned home with the colonists—Manteo to become a loyal friend to the English, Wanchese their implacable enemy.

And John White, an artist who had accompanied Sir Martin Frobisher to Baffin Island in 1577, was selected to draw and paint pictures of the Indians, the flora, and the fauna. So well did the future governor carry out this assignment that to this day no book illustrating Indian life in precolonial days or depicting exploration of North America is complete without reproductions of John White's work.

CHAPTER THREE

The First Colony

On April 9, 1585, the *Tiger, Roebuck, Lyon,* and *Elizabeth*, flying bright pennants and garlanded with flowers, sailed from Plymouth, England, carrying the first English colony ever to be planted in America. They set their course for the coast of newly named Virginia.

"Virginia" then meant a much larger area than the modern state that bears this name; most of the eastern coastal region, from Chesapeake Bay south to "the Land of Florida" was considered part of Virginia.

Sir Richard Grenville, more interested in privateering than in planting a colony, took his time crossing the Atlantic, sailing by the long southern route. He captured two Spanish ships and stopped in Puerto Rico to sell them and to buy a few cattle, hogs, and horses to take to Virginia. He finally reached the coast of Florida in June. The ships then sailed northward, encountering a storm that nearly wrecked them off a point of land they appropriately named Cape Fear.

A few days later their pilot ran *Tiger* aground off the Outer Banks, and as the other ships followed him, they also hit bottom. Only the skilled seamanship of the sailors saved the ships from destruction, and as it was, most of the provisions and supplies were ruined. But the crews managed to get the ships afloat again and continued on their way.

On July 3 they anchored near Roanoke Island, and Grenville sent Manteo and Wanchese by boat to their home on Croatoan Island to announce the arrival of the English.

For eight days the Englishmen explored the country in a pinnace and a longboat. They went up Pamlico Sound and on up the Pamlico and Pungo rivers, looking for a suitable place to settle. Everywhere they were hospitably entertained by the Indians. However, at one Indian village a silver cup was missed by one of the Englishmen. Thinking it had been stolen, Grenville demanded that the Indians return it at once. When it was not immediately restored, Grenville ordered the whole town and its growing corn to be burned. This act marked the beginning of bitter enmity between the English and Indians, which lingered on in North Carolina long after Grenville's expedition had been forgotten.

Grenville sailed his fleet farther north toward Roanoke Island. Here Chief Wingina's brother invited the English to make their colony. Grenville accepted. He landed the colonists, cattle, plants, and all the cargo and supplies that had not been damaged. He had performed his part of the colonizing effort, and after three weeks he sailed away in the *Tiger* to do more privateering on the way home.

The *Roebuck* sailed a few days later, carrying a letter from Governor Ralph Lane to his friend Richard Hakluyt—the first letter ever sent from America to England—telling what a wonderful country Virginia was. Three things were necessary, he decided, to make it desirable for colonization by the English: a better harbor than that at Roanoke, a passage to the South Sea (Pacific Ocean), and gold.

Meanwhile, under the direction of Thomas Hariot, the men built Fort Raleigh and a few dwelling houses at the northern end of the island. They made bricks by mixing the white sand with oyster shells and pressing them in a little hand mold. They sawed thick cedar trees into planks and cut reeds for thatching roofs. Soon a wretched model of an English village was gazing feebly out over the terrible Outer Banks.

Angry over a stolen silver cup, Sir Richard Grenville ordered an Indian village burned. This harsh action embittered the natives and turned them against the first English settlement, which ended in failure.

Sir Francis Drake stopped off at Roanoke in June, 1586, and, at their own request, carried the disgruntled colonists home.

The English planted corn and seeds and set out the sugarcane and plantains they had brought from the West Indies. The tropical plants died at the first frost. Fortunately the winter was mild and the Indians had plentiful supplies; they sold the men food and also built weirs so that the settlers could have a supply of fish. However, it was not the custom of these Indians to store enough corn for the entire winter. They gorged themselves in the fall when they had a plentiful harvest, but when January and February came, they lived on shellfish and edible roots. But the Englishmen, now expecting to get most of their food from the Indians, were not prepared for this annual period of starvation.

In March, 1586, Governor Lane and a few men started out to explore the Chowan River. When they reached an Indian village near the headwaters of that stream, the Indians all ran away, leaving their pets behind. The hungry English killed some of the dogs and roasted them, flavored with sassafras.

Sir Francis Drake to the Rescue

Grenville had promised to send a ship with more supplies in the spring. As March, April, and May passed and no ship appeared, the colonists grew more and more restless. Wanchese had deserted the English and returned to his native tribe, but Manteo continued to live near them and act as Governor Lane's interpreter. Through him Lane learned that Wingina planned to attack and wipe out the English. He had sent word to seven or eight hundred of his subjects and allies to come to Roanoke on the pretense of celebrating a big funeral for his lately deceased father. At the right moment they would fall on the interlopers and destroy them.

In order to weaken the enemy, Wingina gave orders to his people to sell the English no more food and to cut their fish weirs so that the fish would escape. When Wingina built a signal fire, the Indians were to surround and burn the Englishmen's houses and kill each settler as he ran out.

With famine staring them in the face, Governor Lane decided to attack the Indians first. On June 1, in the dark of the moon, Lane and twenty-five men landed at Wingina's mainland village, where they found the chief sitting among his werowances. The English opened fire immediately. Wingina was killed and beheaded. Lane and his men went back to Roanoke, and a week later a message came from Croatoan that a fleet of twenty-three sail had been sighted. Was it the relief fleet or Spaniards?

The fleet was English, but it was not the promised relief. Queen Elizabeth had sent Sir Francis Drake, one of her favorite privateers, to prey on the Spanish in the West Indies. It is probable that Sir Walter Raleigh asked Sir Francis to stop by Virginia and see how his colony at Roanoke was doing, since the ships he had planned to use for relief had been commandeered for the queen's service.

Drake tried to get his ships through the shoals, but they drew too much water, and he had to anchor them about two miles from shore. He had planned to leave supplies with Lane and continue on his way, but on June 13 a hurricane struck the coast and raged for four days. When the storm was over, Governor Lane and his men begged Drake to take all of them home. When he agreed, the 103 surviving colonists abandoned Roanoke, hurried aboard Drake's ships, and departed from Virginia. It was June 18, 1586.

Meanwhile, Raleigh had outfitted his relief ship. Only two days after the colonists departed with Drake, it arrived at Roanoke. Finding no one there but savages, it returned home. Two weeks passed, and in mid-July Sir Richard Grenville turned up with a fleet of several ships. He made a careful search for the colonists and learned from a captured Indian that they had deserted Roanoke. Sir Richard left on the island a token force of eighteen men, to hold the fort for England, and set out to privateer again on his way home.

This colonizing attempt was not altogether unproductive. Samples of three Indian crops were brought home to see how they'd fare in the Old World: *uppawoc*, *pagatour*, and *openauk*. *Uppawoc* (tobacco) was too harsh a variety for English smokers. *Pagatour* (corn) would not grow well in the sunless English climate. But *openauk* (white potato), introduced by Raleigh to Ireland, provided that unhappy land with a staple food that would sustain it for centuries.

CHAPTER FOUR

The Second Colony

Sir Walter Raleigh was bitterly disappointed at the failure of his colony in Virginia, but he was not discouraged. He realized that the first experiment was made with explorers and exploiters, men who thought in terms of passages to the Pacific Ocean and finding gold. It would take plain, hardworking, laboring men—and women—to build a colony in Virginia. In 1586, Sir Walter raised more capital and found new volunteers.

The new colony would be run by a governor and a council appointed by Raleigh, as the old one was. But for this second attempt he offered something to the common people, too: five hundred acres of land for each new colonist plus a voice in the government of the colony.

A number of families volunteered—eighty-nine men, seventeen women, and eleven children, all middle-class English or Irish. Raleigh appointed artist John White governor of "the Cittie of Ralegh in Virginea." Ellinor White Dare, the governor's daughter, decided to accompany her husband and father, even though she was pregnant. Dionyse Harvey took his wife along in the same condition. Manteo, who had made his second trip to England with the colonists who deserted Roanoke, returned again to his Croatoan homeland.

Since the first governor, Ralph Lane, had reported to Raleigh that there was no suitable harbor for large ships near Roanoke—a vital matter if the new colony was to be supplied and protected easily—Sir Walter instructed this second expedition to settle in Chesapeake Bay. They were to stop at Roanoke en route and pick up the men Grenville had left, then continue on to the deep, sheltered, navigable Chesapeake.

On May 8, 1587, a little fleet of the *Lion* plus two smaller vessels whose names are now unknown sailed from Plymouth. Like Grenville, this sea captain was more interested in privateering than in planting a colony, and there was no one to prevent him from having his own way. Although the word of a governor like Lane or White might be law on land, at sea he was helpless to oppose the man who commanded the ships. Accordingly, it was July 22 before the expedition reached Roanoke to pick up Grenville's men.

There was no sign of the Englishmen except a lone skeleton. The fort had been razed and the houses partially burned. Everything was overgrown with gourd and melon vines, and deer grazed among the ruins.

With the aid of Manteo, Governor White found an Indian from whom he learned what had happened. Not long after Grenville left the eighteen men, the mainland Indians attacked them, setting their huts on fire while the Englishmen slept. As they ran out, choking with smoke, poorly dressed and armed, the Indians set on them with bows and tomahawks. Nevertheless, the English fought for an hour or more before deciding to flee. Some managed to escape by boat, but that's all the Indian knew. Presumably the escapees were lost at sea off that treacherous coast.

After learning of the fate of Grenville's men, Governor White directed his captain to sail on to Chesapeake Bay, as Raleigh had provided. The captain refused—it was too late in the summer, he said. White, having no authority over the seamen, could only acquiesce. On July 25, the colonists landed once more on Roanoke.

With the three ships anchored offshore for repairs, White set about organizing his colony. Men were put to work rebuilding Fort Raleigh and repairing the huts. The women washed clothes while the children played on the white sand of the beach.

Indian Relations

Three days after the landing, George Howe, a member of Governor White's council, went crabbing. He did not return. When a party was sent out to look for him, they found him about two miles from Fort Raleigh. He was dead. There were sixteen arrow wounds in his body, and his head had been bashed in.

Governor White did not immediately fly off the handle, as Grenville had done over the silver cup. He knew that the badly outnumbered English needed the Indians' help. Taking Manteo with him, he sailed to Croatoan Island, where Manteo reassured people in their own language and explained that the English had not come to steal corn but to renew old friendship and "live with them as brethren and friendes." It was agreed that Indians and English would hold a conference at Fort Raleigh a day or two later.

When the appointed day arrived, the Indians did not appear. On their way to Fort Raleigh, the Croatoans, functioning on easygoing "Indian time," had found a deserted village of Wingina's people and had stopped to gather the harvest of corn, pumpkins, and tobacco before it fell to the deer and raccoons.

Not knowing this, White was angry and decided he must take revenge for the murder of George Howe. He gathered together his soldiers, and they sailed from Roanoke to the mainland, where Wingina's Indians lived —the ones they suspected, probably with justice, had committed the murder. When they came upon a village filled with Indians, they began haphazard firing, and one Indian was killed. Then the English discovered their mistake. These were not Wingina's men but the friendly Croatoans, who were on their way to the meeting.

This foolish encounter ended more amicably than it deserved to, for the Croatoans remained at peace with the English. But they never completely trusted the white men after that.

Manteo stayed with the English at Roanoke. He taught the men and boys how to kill game with a bow and arrow, to conserve the precious ammunition. Governor White knew of no better reward for the Indian's services than to try to make him into an Englishman. On August 13, the governor christened Manteo into the Church of England and gave him the first and only English peerage ever created on American soil: Lord of Roanoke.

Five days later, on August 18, 1587, Ellinor Dare gave birth to her baby. Virginia Dare was christened with her historic name by her grandfather the following Sunday. A few days later the Harvey child was born, but it is not recorded whether it was a boy or a girl or what it was named.

Repairs to the *Lion* and her consorts had now been completed, and the seamen were anxious to be off privateering again. One of the smaller vessels, the pinnace, would be left behind for the settlers' use. The colonists knew that they needed an agent in London to hurry on supplies and more settlers to Virginia. Governor White preferred to stay with the colony, but the people persuaded him to return to England. On August 27 he sailed, and after many hardships at sea, he reached England in November, 1587.

The Spanish Crisis

In London, White explained to Sir Walter Raleigh that the colonists had arrived at Roanoke too late to plant crops and that the Indians could not be trusted. He begged that supplies and settlers be sent to Roanoke immediately.

This was not so easily done by Sir Walter. All his previous efforts to outfit expeditions of exploration and settlement had left Raleigh almost bankrupt, but he scraped up enough money to buy emergency supplies and arranged to send them out on six or seven ships under Sir Richard Grenville. All the vessels were ready to sail by the end of March, 1588.

At the last minute, however, there came an order from the Queen's Privy Council not to leave the harbor. The Invincible Armada was on its way to conquer England. Every ship of fighting size, and all ammunition and supplies, were commandeered to battle the Spaniards. The colony at Roanoke would have to take care of itself.

Nevertheless, Raleigh persisted and finally obtained permission to send two ships to Roanoke with John White and about fifteen colonists. They left in April, 1588, but as usual the skipper was interested only in privateering. He attacked two large French vessels and was soundly trounced, his ships looted of all supplies before they were released. There was nothing to do but return to England.

In July, the Spanish Armada of 129 ships was sighted in the English Channel. Queen Elizabeth had been able to muster only ninety ships to oppose it, but they were more heavily armed and more skillfully sailed than the Spaniards'. After ten days of ding-dong battling all the way down the channel, the armada was driven off and then destroyed by a great storm.

The crisis past, Sir Walter Raleigh again turned his attention to his colony in America. He knew the colonists had survived the first winter, because a Spanish frigate had reported stopping near Roanoke and seeing them. Still, there was the problem of money.

In desperate straits by now—his £40,000 investment in the New World would easily equal millions of dollars of today's money—he organized the Company of the City of Raleigh to raise more funds. But it was not until two more years had passed that a relief fleet of four large ships could be sent.

On August 18, 1587, the first child of English parents was born in the New World. Three days later the infant was christened by her grandfather, and named for the colony of her birth: Virginia Dare.

Made cautious by bitter experience, Governor White was afraid that the new skipper would go privateering en route as the others had done. Thus he persuaded Raleigh to compel the man to put up a £5,000 bond before leaving England. This made the captain so angry that he left all the new colonists and most of the supplies in England, and despite his bond he set out to privateer anyway.

It was almost five months before the two remaining ships arrived off the coast of Virginia. They dropped anchor August 15, 1590, and what with the capsizing of one boat and the death of six men, it took them all day just to get two rowing craft through the inlet into the sound.

They then rowed toward Roanoke Island, but it was so dark that they overshot Fort Raleigh on their first try and headed instead for the great fire they saw some distance away. The following morning, they visited the place where they had left the colonists—among them Virginia Dare, who if she were alive, would be three years old the next day—and found only the notice carved on a tree: "CROATOAN."

The Lost Colony

The fate of this second colony remained unknown. No further relief expedition was sent. No casual Spanish frigate brought further news of having seen the English settlers. They are known to history as the Lost Colony.

There are many possible explanations of what happened. Perhaps Wingina's people came back and massacred them en masse, or killed some and carried off the others. Perhaps the ferocious Spaniards stopped by again, seized the English, and enslaved them. Or perhaps they became discouraged and decided to try to return home in the pinnace and then got lost at sea.

But the most probable explanation is that they went to Croatoan Island, exactly as their carved tree indicated, and settled among the friendly Croatoans. This tribe migrated from their lonely island in the Outer Banks to the mountains of western North Carolina about 1650, and there remained a strong tradition among them that the Roanoke settlers had become amalgamated to them.

Perhaps so. It's the best thing that could have happened. It would not take long, a generation or two, for all aspects of a different culture to be lost. Virginia Dare's children—supposing she lived to grow up and have children of her own—would be indistinguishable from her fellow tribesmen to a white man seeing them.

The fate of Manteo, the first Indian friend the English had, is also unknown. So the history of North Carolina begins with two romantic people and two unsolvable mysteries.

CHAPTER FIVE

The Indians of Carolina

After John White's little expedition vanished over the Atlantic horizon, the land Raleigh had named Virginia returned to its own affairs. To the Englishmen America had seemed empty. Actually it was well populated—if thinly—by native peoples of many diverse cultures. Before going on to the story of European settlement, let's stop for a moment to see who the first Carolinians were.

Unlike the northern regions of settlement, where English colonists were to encounter Algonkian peoples almost exclusively, Carolina was home to three language groups, or nations, of Indians.

The Fishermen of the Seashore

In the northern and eastern areas, occupying the shores of Albemarle and Pamlico sounds, dwelt a number of Algonkian tribes: the Pasquotank, the Chowanoc, the Coree (or Coramine), the Pamlico, the Machapunga, the Weapemeoc (or Yeopim), the Croatoans, the Secotan, and others.

Algonkians lived in small, scattered, palisaded villages consisting of rectangular houses with open sides and arched roofs covered with white cedar or cypress bark. Mats of woven grass could be lowered to close off the open sides in cold or rainy weather. Living as they did along the seashore, they were great canoers, traveling in their log dugouts (hollowed out with fire and edged tools from the trunks of trees) all over the great Carolina sounds. These were the men Barlowe described as salvaging nails and other metal from the "wrakes" of foundered European ships.

They drank a concoction of water boiled with sassafras and gathered such wild fruits and nuts as mulberries, grapes, cherries, walnuts, chestnuts, hickories, and chinquapins. They cultivated corn, peas, beans, squash, and the native tobacco, but the chief item in their diet was fish.

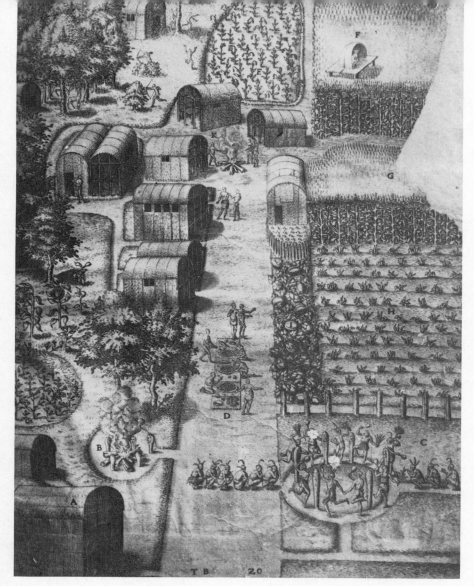

The Algonkian Indians of the Carolina coast lived in small, scattered villages like this one drawn by John White. Their houses (A) were roofed with cedar bark and sided with grass mats that could be raised or lowered. A large fire (B) was kept burning at all times as well as a cooking fire (K). Religious dances (C) also used fire as well as symbolic palmetto fronds and gourds. Several families lived in one house, and eating was communal (D). The artist shows men hunting deer in the nearby forest and children shooing birds from a cornfield (E). Pet dogs have their own shelter (F) behind the garden of corn, squash, pumpkins, and gourds (G, H, and I). Sunflowers grow in another plot to the far left.

They caught fish in several ways, the most sporting of which was torch fishing, carried on at night. The men in one boat would hold a flaming torch over the water, and when the fish came to the surface to investigate the light, men in other canoes would spear them. They also used fish traps or weirs—a line of stakes driven into the bed of a tidal river or bay to form an artificial pond. The entrance, designed like a funnel, allowed the fish to enter but not to leave, and once inside they were easily speared. This trap method was used particularly during the great runs of herring and shad in the spring, when hordes of these fish returned from Labrador to spawn. Once caught, the fish were split open and dried on racks over fires.

Algonkian clothes were of deerskin. In summer, men and women both wore only a short apron about the loins, but in winter they also threw a mantle of hide around their shoulders for warmth. Sometimes a man might wear a cloak made of bird feathers over a netting of fiber. Men and women usually went bareheaded, but occasionally a chief might wear a crown of upright feathers or a cap made from a stuffed eagle's head.

The men clipped their hair close to the scalp at the sides of the head, leaving only a scalp lock—a crest of hair running from the forehead to the nape of the neck. Women wore their hair somewhat longer than men but cut it short about the face. All body and facial hair was plucked out with clamshell tweezers. Both sexes sported tattoos, men on the legs and torso, women on legs, arms, and cheeks.

Seafood was the chief item in the Algonkians' diet. Here artist John White shows several different methods of obtaining it: scooping up crabs with a rake, spearing fish, luring prey into a weir (fish trap). For warmth, fishermen laid sand on the bottom of their boat and built a fire.

The Matriarchs of the River Valleys

Farther inland from the coast-hugging Algonkians and farther south were tribes who spoke an Iroquoian tongue: the Meherrins, the Neusick, the Tuscaroras. These tribes were related culturally and linguistically to such northern Iroquoians as the Huron of the Great Lakes, the Susquehannocks (or Conestogas) of Upper Chesapeake Bay, and the powerful Five Nations of the Mohawk Valley (in present upstate New York). It is traditional among the Tuscaroras that they lived originally in the north but broke off from their kin to resettle in a southern clime.

These Iroquoians lived along the lower reaches of such broad rivers as the Neuse, the Roanoke, the Tar, the Meherrin, the Bear, and the Cape Fear. They did not build large longhouses like their northern relatives but lived in medium-size circular structures of bark over frame. Inside, encircling the walls except by the entrance, were benches for sitting or sleeping. Iroquoian villages were palisaded, for wars and raids were frequent, but the villages seem to have been somewhat larger and more populous than the Algonkian towns.

Iroquoians cultivated much the same crops as the shore people and did a great deal of fishing. Many of them made an annual visit to the shore to catch and dry a store for winter, but such a journey was not essential, for the rivers were full of freshwater fish, and even large sturgeon were caught far upstream. Moreover, the annual run of herring and shad often reached as far inland as these Iroquoian villages. Fish were taken with nets of plant fiber or with bone hooks on lines, or were lured to the bank with lights and harpooned. If a stretch of river formed a small pool, the Iroquoians sometimes poisoned the water with devil's shoestring (*Tephrosia virginiana*), a herb fatal to cold-blooded creatures but harmless to warm-blooded, and gathered in the dead fish as they floated to the surface. Crayfish, a delicacy to these inland peoples, were caught on sharpened reeds driven into the bottom of a stream and baited with partly cooked strips of venison.

The Iroquoians relied less completely on fish than the Algonkians did, however. They were skillful hunters, employing bows of black locust and arrows of cane. The tip was sometimes simply the sharpened cane itself, or the hunter might add a head of sharpened shell or the spur from a turkey cock. Annually, when the leaves fell, entire villages would move to hunting quarters deep in the woods. Sometimes they set the forest on fire, driving all the game in one area into a neck of land between two bodies of water (rather as the fish were lured into the weir), where they were easily slain. So common was this practice of burning that some archaeologists believe it helped create the great Carolina forests of longleaf pine, which thrives in burned-over ground while many other species of tree do not.

Deer and small game were highly desirable, of course, but the prize catch was the bear. The bear was sacred to many Indian peoples, who called him Grandfather and held a feast in his honor whenever one of these beasts was slain. The Iroquoians were no exception. They took pains to beg pardon of the dead animal's spirit and beg it to grace the tribe and come again to feed them. Bear supplied pounds and pounds of sweet meat, heavy fur hide for winter, claws and teeth for necklaces, and—especially if the animal was slain just before he went into hibernation—a great quantity of valuable fat. Bear grease was both eaten and worn, for the Iroquoians dressed their hair with it, rubbed it over their bodies till they glistened (an excellent protection against cold and insect bites), and used it as a base for decorative paints.

When a man wished to dress up, he mixed bear fat with a powder made from a scarlet root—brought at great trouble and expense from the distant mountains. He then rubbed this concoction into his hair to give it a red tinge. He painted his face with it as well, and drew a line of white around one eye, a line of black around the other. Around his neck and dangling from his ears he wore whatever finery he had been able to find, make, buy, or take from an enemy: feathers, bits of shell, animal canine teeth, copper plates, bird wings, bones, beads, stones. Pearls were especially prized, and all Indians treasured and collected them.

The Iroquoians of Carolina lived in a matrilineal society, like their northern kin—that is, a boy belonged to his mother's clan, not his father's. The woman owned the house, her husband being rather a visitor there. When any family matter had to be decided upon, the woman's brothers and maternal uncles discussed the affair and made the decision. The husband was left out of consideration entirely, although he of course took part in his sisters' and nieces' decisionmaking.

Although men served as chieftains, led war parties, and made decisions in all matters that concerned the welfare of the tribe as a whole, it was the women who chose *which* men would govern—a successful and interesting division of power between the sexes.

The Wanderers of the Piedmont

West of the Iroquoians, occupying both the Piedmont region—the rolling clay hills that separate the coastal plain from the mountains—and the well-watered lowlands in what is now South Carolina, were tribes who spoke a language similar to that of the Sioux. These Siouans were divided into two principal groups: the Tutelo or northern branch (the Manahoac, the Monacan, the Monahassano or Nahyssan, the Occaneechi, the Saponi) and the Catawba or southern branch (the Cheraw, the Sissipahaw, the Waccamaw, the Winyaw, the Waxhaw, the Congaree, the Keyauwee, the Sugree, the Yamasee, the Pedee, the Santee, the Wateree, the Cape Fear, the Eno).

Their homeland in the foothills not only was not flat like that of the other two language groups but had poorer soil. Consequently, although they relied to some extent on the women's agriculture—one Siouan cornfield was reported to be seven miles long—the men were primarily hunters and warriors. Indeed, their reputation in both these roles has long outlasted their power. In the nineteenth century, famed ethnologist Henry Rowe Schoolcraft wrote that the Catawba had "a fixed character for indomitable courage and consummate art in forest life." And a contemporary white observer described the Tutelo as "tall, likely men, having great plenty of buffaloes, elks, and bears, with every sort of deer amongst them, which strong food makes large, robust bodies."

The Siouans' ordinary hunting ground ranged from the Shenandoah Valley in the north nearly to the Savannah River in the south, but when game was scarce, hunting parties sometimes traveled incredible distances—to Florida, to the Great Lakes, to New York, to Kentucky. These incursions into the hunting lands of other tribes naturally got the Siouans into trouble, but they didn't mind. They were on bad terms with everyone * and glad of it. They enjoyed war.

Some Siouans practiced head flattening (as did the Iroquoian Tuscarora). They would weight a baby's skull with a bag of sand or a buckskin-covered block of wood, over a period of time, until the soft little skull gradually became flattened to an unnatural shape. Such a deformed head obviously added to the frightening appearance of an adult warrior, and indeed many other Indians regarded the Siouans as barbaric for indulging in such practices.

But these tribesmen had mastered many peaceable arts too. Containers were a great problem with southern tribes, who lacked the versatile and easily worked birchbark. (The paper birch does not grow south of Pennsylvania.) So the Siouan women wove bags of animal hair. They made baskets of oak splints, dying some strands with plant juices in order to obtain colors and patterns in the weave. They carved bowls from tupelo gum wood ("bowl gum," the English called this tree) and made gracefully shaped and artfully designed pipe bowls.

The clay that underlay the Piedmont made pottery an important art for Siouan peoples. Since no Indian cultures, not even such high civilizations

---

* Except, ironically, with white men. Indeed, the Catawba, barring one small early lapse, fought on the side of the whites in every conflict up to and including World War II. But that came later.

as the Inca and the Aztec, had invented the potter's wheel, pots had to be modeled by other methods. One was to press the clay over a mold of some kind—usually the bottom of an old bowl or a basket—a technique that worked only with bowls or other flare-topped crockery. A more useful method was coiling. Wet clay was molded into a long rope, which was then coiled around and around on itself to form the vessel's bottom and sides. The potter smoothed her material as she worked; when it had reached the shape and evenness she wanted, she might decorate the outside with painted or incised designs. When the pot was ready, it was baked, sometimes simply in the hot Carolina sun. Sometimes it was inverted on a rock, and a fire built alongside. Then the potter would cover both the pot and fire with green sticks to form a primitive oven. Whichever method she used, when the baking was done, the potter had a vessel that would hold water and could be used to cook in. By these and similar methods pottery was made in the American Southeast as much as four thousand years ago— longer than in any other region of North America.

The Sport-Loving Men of the Mountains

The last group of Indians in Carolina were mountain people, occupying about two hundred villages in a region of some forty thousand square miles, covering parts of what are now western North Carolina, northern Georgia, and eastern Tennessee. They spoke an Iroquoian language, and we know them as the Cherokee.

In North Carolina the Appalachians reach their greatest height, swelling higher and higher in rugged green beauty until they culminate in Mount Mitchell, 6,684 feet, the loftiest point east of the Mississippi. Fall stipples the mountain flanks of this beautiful area orange and vermilion and gold; damp spring adorns the high trails with flowering rhododendron, azalea, dogwood. But life was not easy in this difficult, remote land, and it took a lively and ingenious people to thrive there. And that is exactly what the early Cherokee were.

In shape, the round Cherokee houses were similar to those of their lowland cousins, but bark trees were scarce in the mountains, so the house builder had to make do with other materials for sheathing. He started his task by digging a circular depression in the ground, in the center of which he set up four sturdy posts. Around the edge of the depression he drove in long hickory poles, bringing the slender upper ends together in the middle and lashing them to the supporting posts with fiber rope. That was his framework. Next he took smaller sticks and wove them in and out around the hickory poles, until the house looked like nothing so much as a huge, upside-down basket. Finally a plaster of clay and grass was daubed over the basketwork, and mats of grass were laid on top to protect the plaster from rain and wind. As a building technique it was surprisingly similar to the wattle-and-daub construction so popular in sixteenth-century England, except it was somewhat less sturdy. Wind, rain, and winter snow steadily crumbled the clay, and a house owner had to repair and replaster regularly.

Like others, the Cherokee lived by a combination of agriculture and hunting, with hunting perhaps dominant. They were not unwarlike, either, and they regarded both the Siouan peoples and their distant relatives the Tuscarora as inveterate enemies. In 1656, they defeated the Algonkian Pamunkeys and their English allies in "perhaps the bloodiest Indian battle ever fought in Virginia." When they weren't raiding their lowland neighbors, the Cherokee fought among themselves, one village against another distant one. Like all Iroquoian peoples, they killed prisoners of war by torture, and every warrior expected to die in agony if he was captured.

Sometimes this intervillage warfare was converted into sport. In a single-opponent game called chunkey, two players bowled a concave-sided disk ahead of them and tried to land a sharpened stick near where the disk stopped rolling. The man whose stick landed closest won—rather like the scoring in boccie, or Italian bowling. But the game at which the Cherokee

Three Cherokee chiefs, resplendent in paint and finery, on a ceremonial visit. One carries a peace belt of wampum in one hand, a warlike tomahawk in the other.

seemed to let off the most steam was the southern version of lacrosse, aptly nicknamed the Little Brother of War.

The Great Lakes Indians and the northern Iroquoians played the game with a single stick having a crook at the top (hence the French name *la crosse*, "the crozier"), which held a small net. The Cherokee played with *two* sticks, each ending in a loop like a tiny tennis racket strung with squirrel gut. The ball was of deerskin, tightly packed and covered with hide. The object of the game was to whack, sling, sock, thump, knock, bang, shoot, or otherwise impel this ball through the opponent's goal posts. There was no such thing as a foul, and hundreds of men took part on each side. The following is from a dumbfounded eyewitness account of one such game.

> In these desperate struggles for the ball, hundreds of strong young Indian athletes were running together and leaping, actually over each other's heads and darting between their adversary's legs, tripping and throwing, and foiling each other in every possible manner, and every voice raised to its highest key in shrill yelps and barks! . . . These obstructions often meet desperate resistance, which terminate in violent scuffles and sometimes in fisticuffs; when their sticks are dropped and the parties are unmolested whilst settling matters between themselves. . . .

As time went on, the Little Brother of War came to be considered part of religious and social functions, usually related to such annual ceremonies as the Green Corn Dance and the Planting. Before a game, team members abstained from sexual contact for several days, painted and decorated themselves, took part in religious purifications, and made spiritual offerings of tobacco. Ethnologists believe that such expressions of spiritual and physical unity among members of one clan or one village helped to strengthen their sense of power and oneness.

In the long tragedy of Indian history, the story of the Cherokee would be perhaps the most tragic. But that lay in the far distant future. For now they remained happy and secure in their mountain fastnesses, hardly knowing—and certainly not caring—that the white-sailed ships of the English had returned to Virginia and that this time they would stay.

32

CHAPTER SIX

South Virginia

After Queen Elizabeth died on March 24, 1603, James I, a mean, narrow-minded Scot, came to the throne. He disliked Sir Walter Raleigh and soon saw to it that Raleigh was stripped of his sources of income, convicted of treason on trumped-up charges, imprisoned in the Tower of London for thirteen years, and finally beheaded. But even while the great Elizabethan languished in the Tower, his dream of an English colony in the New World was coming true—under other auspices.

In 1606, James issued a charter to a group of merchants calling themselves the London Company, which authorized them to establish settlements in America between 34 and 45 degrees of latitude (approximately Cape Fear to Halifax, Nova Scotia). The merchants enlisted would-be settlers, and in December three small ships set sail from London. Held up by bad weather, the expedition did not arrive in America until spring. On May 13, 1607, they landed at a site along a navigable river in latitude 37. They named their new settlement Jamestown.

The Vital Crop

Two things made Jamestown succeed where Roanoke had failed: strong, sustained support from its backers, and tobacco.

The Spanish and Portuguese in their southern colonies had long since adopted the Indians' habit of smoking, and by the end of the sixteenth century they had carried the habit and the leaf to the far corners of the earth. Smoking was introduced into England in the 1560's, and one Englishman who took to the new fad of "drinking smoke" was Sir Walter Raleigh. There is a famous story, whether true or not, that Raleigh's servant entered his master's room one day and, seeing puffs of smoke rise above Raleigh's chair, hastily dowsed him with a bucket of water.

The first North American tobacco sent to England was too harsh for Europeans, but the enterprising Virginians obtained seeds of a milder

Caribbean variety, experimented with methods of curing it, and in 1614 sent their first cargo of leaf to London. It was a solid success. Overnight, men had a reason for settling in the New World—to grow rich by raising tobacco. A steady stream of adventurers began to flow from England to Virginia.

Tobacco has a serious drawback, however: It slowly destroys the fertility of the soil on which it is grown. A man might settle on a promising piece of ground, clear it, plant and harvest crops for a few years, and then find his yield dropping off—every season a little less leaf of a little poorer quality. In those early days, when grants of land were readily obtained by an active, energetic man, the easiest thing to do was find another promising piece of ground.

Land along the rivers was most highly valued. Not only was bottom land richest, from the alluvial deposits left by the flowing water, but the location gave the planter easy access to market. Rivers and creeks were the colonists' first roads.

Consequently, when one tobacco farm began to give out, a planter looked around for another piece of bottom land to settle on. In this fash-

Tobacco was what made settlement in Virginia possible. As fields became exhausted, planters followed the river valleys into the region they called first South Virginia, later Albemarle.

ion, settlement began to creep up one Virginia river after another. When the James and the York had been settled, Virginians began to look longingly southward.

"Most fertile, gallant rich soil," one of them wrote of the region that is now North Carolina, "flourishing in all the abundance of nature . . . a serene air and a temperate clime . . . and stately timber of all sorts. . . ." A man could raise marvelous crops down there in "South Virginia." The land was level, well watered by broad tidal rivers, covered with a light sandy loam that could be easily cleared, easily cultivated. But . . .

Like tobacco, North Carolina had a drawback: its geography. Its coastal plain, though broad and flat and fertile, was virtually inaccessible by sea. The Outer Banks, that great arc of sandbar 320 miles long, prevented deep-keeled cargo vessels from entering the sounds. Therefore, what could a farmer do with his tobacco crop after it was grown? Transship it in small boats to a deep-water port? They had no need of such desperate measures yet.

So for many decades settlers forgot about "South Virginia." A few traders ventured into the region to barter with the Indians for pelts. Occasionally an adventuresome hunter or trapper explored its forests and rivers. But for the most part, the area remained unsettled by white men.

Meanwhile, the rest of the North American seaboard began to show more and more English settlements: 1620 Massachusetts, 1623 New Hampshire, 1633 Connecticut, 1634 Maryland, 1636 Rhode Island. In 1638, a party of Swedes settled in Delaware, and by 1640 there were Dutch settlements in what are now New York and New Jersey. A few years after these last settlements were established, Virginians at last began to move south.

The First White Men in North Carolina

In 1648, a group of Virginia planters bought a large tract of land on the Chowan River, which rises in Virginia and flows south into Albemarle Sound. Five years later, one Roger Green was granted ten thousand acres of the same valley, to be divided among one hundred settlers. It is unknown whether these first two grants actually resulted in emigration into "South Virginia," but in the decade 1650–60 permanent settlement did begin to dot the region between the present Virginia line and Albemarle Sound. This far northeastern corner of the state thus became the first section to be settled and has since been nicknamed the Cradle of North Carolina.

An important early settler was George Durant. After exploring for two years for the piece of land he wanted, Durant found it in an area between the Perquimans and Little rivers—an area still called Durant's Neck. On March 1, 1661, he bought the tract from Kilcocanen, chief of the Weapemeoc Indians. The deed to this property still exists, the oldest grant of land in North Carolina for which there is documentary proof.

While these Virginians were taking root in the Albemarle region, a group of Massachusetts men were attempting to settle the Cape Fear region in southern North Carolina. Forming an association to explore the warmer parts of the American coastline, this group of Yankees set out to find a gentler climate than their own in which to graze cattle. In 1661, they landed at Cape Fear. They turned their cattle loose but did not remain themselves. When they finally moved out, some time before 1663, they left behind "a writing" attached to a post, "the Contents thereof tended . . . to the disparagement of the land about the said River." Neither the soil nor the harbor were fit for settlement, claimed the Yankees.

At about the same time that the Yankees were contemplating a settlement in the area south of Virginia, a group of men in Barbados were also looking for new places to settle. Most of them were refugees from the English Civil War who disliked life on these Caribbean islands. They hired William Hilton with his ship *Adventure* to explore the Carolina coast. In two voyages, he examined the Cape Fear region, which he reached the second time, in 1663, only after weathering one of the violent storms for which that coast is famous. Having heard the story of the New Englanders, Hilton expected to find cattle running wild, but not one could be found. Evidently the Indians had found and killed them for food.

Sixty days after leaving Cape Fear, Hilton arrived back at Barbados, where he wrote a glowing report of his voyage, *A Relation of a Discovery Lately Made on the Coast of Florida*. In it he strongly denounced the New Englanders' report and so encouraged the would-be emigrants that they sent off a first installment of colonists in May, 1664.

These Barbadians established themselves at the mouth of a creek known as Old Town Creek and called their settlement Charles Town. They struggled along here for a year and a half alone. They built houses and forts of local material and tried to make their colony as productive as Virginia. They were still dependent on imports for much of their food and all of their clothing and tools. But they planted corn and cottonseed, which they had brought from Barbados, and they cut the tall trees for timber and shipped it home. They also caught some Indian children and shipped them to Barbados as slaves.

The Indians were fearful of the white men's guns, so they took revenge by killing the Barbadians' cattle. By the end of their second summer in Carolina, the white men were short of clothing, food, and ammunition. They lived from day to day in hopes of relief from home.

A second group of Barbadians joined the first, but they were not the hoped-for relief expedition. Ninety Barbadians had set out in the summer of 1665 to make a settlement in what is now South Carolina, but a storm carried them north to the mouth of the Cape Fear River, and they ended by joining the Barbadians at Charles Town.

Help was on the way, however. An official governor, Colonel Sir John Yeamans, appointed from England, was leading an expedition to back up the first self-selected settlers. With a little fleet consisting of a frigate, a sloop, and a flyboat named *Sir John*, the governor set out for the Cape Fear River in October, 1665.

The expedition had just reached the mouth of the Cape Fear when one of Carolina's famous storms came up. The *Sir John* was swept onto the Outer Banks, where she was broken to pieces by the waves. The crew managed to escape, but the provisions, clothing, ammunition, and cannon were all lost. The governor nevertheless managed to land the rest of his colonists and himself at Charles Town, where he renamed the region Clarendon County after his English patron.

In December, 1665, Governor Yeamans held an assembly, at which the Barbadians were allowed to state their grievances. There were many. Rents were too high. The method of surveying land and marking out individual plots was not satisfactory. Taxes were unreasonable. Yeamans soon tired of his difficult job and abandoned the settlement, leaving a young man named John Vassall in charge.

Vassall was conscientious and did his best, but he found it impossible to keep the colonists together. Many began to leave. One group journeyed on foot to Albemarle, and neither his arguments nor his authority could stop them. Finally, when a ship stopped at Charles Town, he asked the captain to take them all away, to Boston or Virginia or wherever they wanted to go. Thus in September, 1667, Charles Town on the Cape Fear River was abandoned.

Three years later, another settlement with the same name was made about 150 miles south of Cape Fear. It faced on a magnificent harbor formed by two rivers, which the new settlers named the Ashley and the Cooper, and it had few of the geographical difficulties that plagued settlements farther north. It soon began to thrive. Today we call it Charleston, South Carolina.

But Charles Town on the Cape Fear made its historical mark on the history of Carolina too, for the appointment of Sir John Yeamans as its governor was the first effective action of the region's new rulers. Carolina—like Maryland before her and New Jersey, New York, and Pennsylvania after her—had been named a proprietary province.

CHAPTER SEVEN

A Grant Made in Jest

Actually, Carolina was given away twice. On October 20, 1629, Charles I granted to his attorney-general, Sir Robert Heath, territory between 31 and 36 degrees of latitude. (In modern terms, this means most of North Carolina, all of South Carolina, and nine tenths of Georgia.) This vast land was to be called Carolana, from *Carolus*, the Latin for "Charles."

Heath had full power to "people, plant, and dispose" of his colony, but beyond making a few half-hearted grants of territory to English acquaintances, he altogether failed to settle it. The friends were equally indifferent to their new acquisition, so it was not until Virginians began to infiltrate the region that there were any white "plantations" (that is, settlements) at all within the bounds of Carolana.

Eventually, the English Civil War having intervened and swept away many old notions, the Heath grant was felt to have lapsed.

Then one day in April, 1663, King Charles II was enjoying the fresh air in the garden at Hampton Court, accompanied by his ever-present, sad-eyed little spaniels. Charles had been restored to the English throne partly through the efforts of a few loyal friends, and on this day they approached him with a petition that would repay them for their services—a grant of land in America.

The petitioners had drawn up a lengthy draft, in which they piously declared that they wanted the grant for the purpose of propagating the Gospel among the heathen. The Merrie Monarch, knowing that their purpose was more mercenary than religious, looked each man solemnly in the face for a moment, then burst into loud laughter. His audience had little choice but to join in. The king then picked up one of his shaggy little spaniels with large, meek eyes and held it out at arm's length toward the petitioners.

"Good friends," he said, "here is a model of piety and sincerity which it might be wholesome for you to copy." Then, tossing the dog to Lord

Eight aristocratic Englishmen were named the "true and absolute Lords Proprietors" of Carolina by this charter, issued by Charles II on April 3, 1663. They and their descendants remained virtual kings of the area until 1729, when the monarch bought it back.

Clarendon, he added, "There, Hyde, is a worthy prelate. Make him archbishop of the domain which I shall give you."

Thus, on April 3, 1663, Charles II granted the Lords Proprietors the territory of Carolina, now spelled with an *i*, with the same boundaries as those in the former Heath grant.

For all the king's sardonic humor, there were four serious reasons for issuing a charter for a colony in the New World: 1) the propagation of the Christian faith, 2) the "enlargement" of the king's domain, 3) the expansion of English trade, and 4) the increase of the wealth and prestige of the proprietors.

The Eight Lords Proprietors

"The true and absolute Lords Proprietors" received all the territory "lying between Lucke Island and River Saint Matthias," or 36 and 31 degrees north latitude, to be held "in free and common socage [land tenure]" for an annual rent of twenty marks. A mark was worth two thirds of a pound, or 13s 4d; hence this annual rent came to a little over £13.

The Lords Proprietors were eight clever men of business, already rich and powerful but hoping, by means of their splendid grant of land, to become richer and more powerful still. The eight, who have left their names all over the North and South Carolina maps, are as follows:

Edward Hyde, Earl of Clarendon, lord chancellor of England and vigorous opponent of religious toleration, had long supported both Charles I and Charles II while in exile. (Hyde County and Clarendon in Columbus County, North Carolina.)

George Monck, general under Cromwell during the Commonwealth and later his successor, abandoned the Parliamentary cause to support the Restoration of Charles II, who in gratitude created him duke of Albemarle. (Albemarle Sound and Albemarle in Stanly County, North Carolina.)

Sir Anthony Ashley Cooper, Baron Ashley and, after 1672, earl of Shaftesbury, began his career as a follower of Charles I but soon changed sides and served in the Parliamentary forces. When the climate of the nation began to favor Charles's return, Ashley Cooper was one of those sent to bring the exiled king home again. (The Ashley and Cooper rivers in South Carolina.)

William Craven, earl of Craven, a soldier who had fought in several different Continental armies, remained in service to the Bohemian queen while civil war raged in England. However, he supplied both Charles I and Charles II with large sums of money, and after the Restoration he was rewarded for this with an earldom and a seat on the Privy Council. (Craven in Rowan County, North Carolina.)

Sir George Carteret, naval officer and lieutenant-governor of the Isle of Jersey, where he was born, remained loyal to the crown throughout the upheavals of 1642–60, and at the Restoration he returned from exile with his king. Carteret, later a proprietor of New Jersey (the colony was named for his birthplace), was once described by a colleague as "passionate, ignorant and not too honest." (Carteret County, North Carolina.)

Sir John Colleton, a Barbadian planter and slave trader, was another who had played both sides of the Civil War. (Colleton County, South Carolina.)

The Berkeley brothers, John Lord Berkeley of Stratton and Sir William Berkeley, were both stout Royalists, waiting out the Restoration in retirement. Lord Berkeley, later with Carteret a proprietor of New Jersey, had served loyally on the king's side during the war, and at the Restoration he was appointed to the Admiralty staff. Sir William, one of Charles I's last colonial appointments before being stripped of his power, was royalist governor of Virginia. Although deposed by Parliamentary commissioners in 1652, he was restored to his office in 1660 and still held the governorship at the time that the grant of Carolina was issued. (Berkeley County, South Carolina.)

One of the first things the eight did was to appoint Yeamans governor of the ill-fated expedition to Charles Town on the Cape Fear River. Another was to petition for more land.

According to the Heath grant, upon which the later one was based, the northern boundary of Carolina ran through Albemarle Sound and hence did not include the only permanent settlements in the granted region—the two thousand or so persons who had by then moved south from Virginia. When the proprietors found out about this, they asked for a new charter that would include the settled area. Charles agreed, and in 1665 he extended the boundaries of Carolina thirty minutes northward, making the new boundary 36 degrees 30 minutes north, a few seconds short of the present line.

A third action on the part of the Lords Proprietors was to advertise for more settlers. Their lordships preferred "seasoned" people (men and women who had already lived some years in the colonies and had survived the fevers and other misfortunes that plagued newcomers), and since Barbados and New England were the most thickly settled of English colonies, they particularly sought them in those two regions.

Land was to be granted on the basis of head rights, as in Virginia. The "undertaker" (the person who "undertook" to settle a piece of ground) received one hundred acres for himself and his family, and additional acreage for each servant he brought with him—fifty acres for a man, thirty for a woman. These were bond servants, of course, and had to serve their masters for a certain term of years. But when their indentures expired, they were to receive acreage of their own—ten acres for a man, six for a woman.

For the governing of this region, the proprietors drew up the Concessions and Agreements, a kind of rough-draft constitution, promising prospective colonists freedom of conscience and an assembly of freeholders as a lawmaking body. They also notified the people of Carolina that they intended to charge quitrents of a halfpenny an acre, payable in specie.

The Great Deed

Sir William Berkeley, ordered to appoint Albemarle's first governor, chose William Drummond, a wealthy Scot who owned a large plantation in Virginia.

Drummond's sympathies were all with the settlers. Being independent-minded himself, he interfered little with their freedom of action. The first assembly of the Albemarle legislature met during his governorship, early in 1665, and passed a few simple laws, including one limiting the production of tobacco. Then, apparently with the governor's approval, the del-

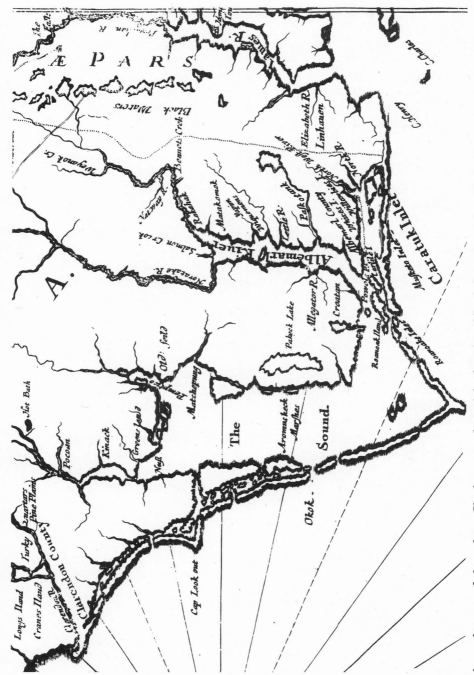

An early map of the colony Charles granted to eight favorites. North is to the right. Albemarle, as the northern area of settlement was called, was the region between "Albemarle River" (now the Sound) and the dotted line that represents Virginia's border.

egates drew up a petition to the Lords Proprietors on the subject of quitrents.

Halfpenny an acre was too much to pay, said the Carolina legislators. Their poor farms, newly wrenched from the wilderness, could not produce such a surplus—especially since their tobacco was also subject to the high costs of transshipment. Besides, Virginia paid only a farthing an acre, half of a halfpenny—and paid it in produce instead of the hard-to-come-by cash. How could the Lords Proprietors hope to induce men to settle in their province, said the petition, if they made such demands of them?

Quitrents were a hangover from the days of feudalism. Under a feudal system, all land tenure was by service. A peasant retained his farm by working his master's land for so many days a year, a knight retained his manor by fighting his lord's wars for so many days a year, and so on. But as civilization in Europe grew more complex and sophisticated, this simple system broke down, and men began to substitute a money payment in lieu of working or fighting. That's what a quitrent was—a payment of money in order to be "quit" of performing services.

In practice, quitrents served somewhat the same function as modern property taxes. A landowner today is assessed a certain sum every year to cover local services: fire and police protection, schools, garbage collection, highway and street maintenance, and so on. But having paid his share, the modern landowner does receive all these services. The colonial quitrent payer, on the other hand, received few roads, no schools, no public health services, and only a modicum of protection against Indians and pirates.

Quitrents covered the governor's salary and those of his councillors, assemblymen, and a few other colonial officials. When these costs were paid, the balance went straight into the pockets of the Lords Proprietors. Therefore, when the Carolina quitrent was raised, there was only one purpose in mind—enrichment of eight aristocrats in England at the expense of the hardworking settler in the colony.

When the assembly's petition reached the Lords Proprietors in England, they took their time thinking it over. Three years, in fact. Then late in 1667 word came that the Cape Fear settlement had been abandoned, and the eight realized that the Albemarle people were the only settlers they had. Perhaps, for the time being, it was best to conciliate them. They drew up and signed an agreement that quitrents in Carolina would be on the same basis as Virginia's.

This document, called by Carolinians the Great Deed, was received in Albemarle with general rejoicing. They thought that the problem of quitrents was solved for good and all, and that their future under the protection of the Lords Proprietors was secure and assured.

Instead, this was to be only the first of many squabbles over quitrents, a battle that lasted as long as Carolina remained a proprietary colony.

CHAPTER EIGHT

The Fundamental Constitutions of Carolina

In 1666, Sir Anthony Ashley Cooper, Lord Ashley, soon to become Lord Shaftesbury, met a thirty-four-year-old Oxford scholar named John Locke. The two men found that they shared an avid interest in civil and religious liberty, and since young Locke had nothing else to do at the moment, Ashley set him to working up a constitution for an ideal colony. Like his seven colleagues, Ashley regarded the Concessions and Agreements—and probably the Great Deed as well—as a mere makeshift.

Locke, who in time would come to be regarded as one of England's greatest political philosophers, was the originator of such daring new doctrines as the separation of executive and legislative powers and the right of a people to overthrow a tyrannical government. He believed in freedom of worship and freedom of speech, and he held that private property must be protected against the ravages of greedy and irresponsible rulers. But as a child of his age, he also believed in a hierarchic social system, in which wealthy and powerful men of the "better sort" ran things benevolently for the well-being of the "lower sort." He also knew astonishingly little about conditions in America.

Consequently, on the basis of an artificially contrived aristocracy—"that we may avoid erecting a numerous Democracy"—Locke set up the government of Carolina. The document "establishing" it was issued by the proprietors on March 11, 1669, as the Fundamental Constitutions.

The three counties of Albemarle, Clarendon, and Craven were declared to consist of 480,000 acres each—although Carolina had scarcely been explored and mapped, let alone surveyed. Each proprietor, holding the title "seignior," was to own a 12,000-acre tract in each county, 36,000 acres in all apiece. Since the proprietors could not be expected to live in such an outlandish wilderness themselves, they were to send to each county a subordinate aristocrat bearing the title "landgrave" (German for a certain

Philosopher John Locke was assigned to draw up the Fundamental Constitutions of Carolina. Although a daring thinker on political subjects, Locke did not understand colonial conditions, and his blueprint for a rigid aristocratic society soon fell into abeyance.

grade of count). Each landgrave would own four tracts of 12,000 acres each, 48,000 acres in all. Below the landgraves were men titled "caciques" (Spanish for Indian chiefs), each with two tracts, 24,000 acres in all apiece. Then came "lords of manors" with 3,000 to 12,000 acres apiece, and finally "freeholders," men holding any grant smaller than 3,000 acres. Ownership of fifty acres was declared the minimum requirement for voting privileges, and these "lower sorts" were expected to revere and obey their betters.

At the head of this elaborate structure stood the Lords Proprietors, who appointed governors and hereditary nobles, approved or disallowed laws (there was no overriding a proprietary veto), and acted as a court of appeals from the provincial courts.

The governor was appointed to an indefinite term, and he in turn appointed his council of six members and presided over it. He appointed all judges and granted all military commissions. He could remove local officials at will and could pardon men convicted of crimes. He could dissolve the assembly if he did not approve of its actions, and he could veto any law it passed before it reached the proprietors. He was to be the real governing power in Carolina. He even had a seat in the assembly, which was to consist of him, the hereditary nobility, and all freeholders owning five hundred acres or more.

On paper the Fundamental Constitutions was a neat and orderly frame of government. If the Carolina settlers had been dolls and their colony a toy countryside, the proprietors might have been able to arrange them exactly like Locke's blueprint. But they were human beings and independent of spirit, and their land was raw new country where a man's ownership of a piece of ground depended less on a parchment signed in London than on what he could clear and plant with his own labor. Men like that don't want to be ruled by others, even of the "better sort."

From the first, the assembly refused to agree to Locke's plan, and it simply never took hold. The proprietors created over the years three seigniors, twenty-six landgraves, and thirteen caciques, but most of these titles died with the men to whom they'd been granted. Freedom of worship had been guaranteed by the Fundamental Constitutions, but within a year that was modified by a declaration in favor of establishing the Church of England. The assembly soon came to resemble that in other colonies—an elective body of representatives from every "precinct" (subdivision of a county) sitting as a lower house while the governor's Grand Council served as an upper. And so it went.

Three times in the next thirty years the proprietors revised and tried to revive the Fundamental Constitutions, but by 1700 it was generally understood that the philosophical experiment had failed.

Rogues' Haven

The province that King Charles had so blithely bestowed on his eight favorites was so far a land of loners. The settlers of Albemarle did not want to live together in villages, preferring to be separated from one another by miles of forest or water. A fiercely independent lot, they had not tried to form their own government, because they didn't want any government. Nor did they want any organized religion. They just wanted to be left alone to raise their corn, hogs, and children, to grow and ship tobacco when they needed a little cash.

Many early settlers lived in one-room houses, wood frame covered with bark slabs. Since the ground did not freeze hard and heave as it did farther north, they laid the log frames right on the ground and left the earth itself for a floor, to become hard-packed with use. A fireplace of clayed sticks provided cooking and heating facilities, and the few necessary items of furniture were made from split shakes or slices of log.

Few of the "better sort" were attracted to this backwoodsy life. Albemarle soon came to seem like the disreputable backyard of Virginia, offering shelter to runaway servants and Negro slaves, to men who had fallen into debt or afoul of the law. "Rogues' Haven," Virginians called it contemptuously.

The proprietors only blackened this raffish reputation further. In an effort to encourage lagging migration, they offered some handsome new concessions: A new settler would be immune to civil suit (for collection of debt, for instance) for his first five years; he and his sweetheart could be married by a civil official and need not wait for a clergyman (a scarce commodity) to reach his remote settlement; only a resident of Carolina could "truck and trade" with the Indians—men from other colonies were barred. This naturally drained still more "theaves" from their Virginia masters.

Prospective English, Barbadian, and New Englander settlers were not told this about Carolina, however. Instead, the proprietors fell back on employing writers to produce enticing pamphlets:

> The Heavens shine upon this famous Country the soveraign Ray of health [trilled one of their hacks in the tone of real-estate promoters in every age]; and has blest it with a serene Air, and a lofty Skie, that defends it from Noxious Infection; nor is there any known Distemper. . . . A salubrious Air to the sick, and diseased; and a generous retirement to necessitous and abject Families.

And yet, despite all this hard-sell campaign for settlers, men hung back. The son of Sir John Colleton early lamented that it was "a very difficult matter to gitt a man of worth and trust to go thither." Carolina would not appeal to prospective colonists until some of the confusion regarding quitrents and land tenure had been cleared away. For the Fundamental Constitutions had stated flatly that the Lords Proprietors might raise quitrents to a penny an acre—four times what was paid in Virginia.

CHAPTER NINE

Governor Trouble

After the expiration of William Drummond's term as governor of Albemarle, one Samuel Stephens was appointed. When he died in 1669, the council chose as governor Peter Carteret, a relative of Lord Proprietor Sir George Carteret. Carteret arrived with instructions from their lordships to raise quitrents from a farthing to halfpence an acre.

Indignation swept through the rough-and-tumble new colony. Halfpence was better than a penny but still twice the rate paid in Virginia! The Speaker of the Assembly showed Governor Carteret the Great Deed, which contained the promise of the Lords Proprietors that Carolina quitrents would be on the same basis as those in Virginia.

Carteret sent a copy of this document to London, to remind their lordships of this pledge, and for the moment they relented.

Plantation Duty

Meanwhile, the long arm of England was starting to take a tighter grip on its overseas colonies. During the Commonwealth and again in 1660, Parliament had passed Navigation Acts, which decreed that it was illegal for colonists to sell their products directly to any country other than England or to ship them in a foreign ship. Then in 1673 came legislation to regulate intercolonial trade. This act imposed on certain "enumerated articles"—foremost among them tobacco—a customs duty when shipped from one colony to another. This intercolonial tariff was called plantation duty.

Plantation duty worked a particular hardship on Carolina. Because of its shallow, tricky coast, only small vessels could reach Albemarle to load the colonists' tobacco. Consequently, to get their tobacco to market the Carolinians were heavily dependent on New England, where men built and sailed smaller ships than the English. Paying plantation duty on top of all the other difficulties made tobacco hardly worth the raising. And tobacco was the only possible cash crop.

Some Carolinians resorted to evasion and shipped leaf out in barrels labeled "bait for New England fishermen." Others simply refused to pay. Anger over plantation duty became confused in men's minds with anger over the proprietors' greed. (Remember: Quitrents were paid to the Lords Proprietors, plantation duty to the Crown.) Parties began to form in the colony—those who opposed the proprietors and plantation duty on the one hand versus those who supported both.

The antiproprietorial party consisted chiefly of the earliest and most substantial planters, who bitterly resented the Lords Proprietors and their assumption of authority. Such men as George Durant of Durant's Neck felt that, since they had won their estates by dint of backbreaking labor and daring, it was unjust for eight royal favorites to be granted the profits rightly due to those who had actually braved the wilderness.

They longed to be rid of proprietorial rule altogether, but at first they plotted only against plantation duty. When Governor Peter Carteret resigned in 1673, it seemed that luck was coming their way. For the retiring governor appointed as his successor one John Jenkins, a leader with Durant of the antiproprietorial party.

Jenkins, ordered by the government in London to appoint an official collector of plantation duty, named a wealthy, antiproprietorial friend, Valentine Byrd. Under Byrd's and Jenkins' benign rule, plantation duty went uncollected, and such large planters as Durant, Surveyor-General John Culpeper, and Jenkins himself waxed rich.

Everything went well with the antiproprietorial party for two years. Then Jenkins took revenge on a political enemy named Thomas Miller by having him jailed on a charge of "treasonable utterances." Miller was an apothecary, often drunk, and a member of the proprietorial party. An influential friend of Miller's, one Thomas Eastchurch, was speaker of the colonial assembly. Eastchurch induced the assembly to vote Governor Jenkins out of office.

But this attempt did not work, for the assembly had no authority to pick and choose governors. So when Miller managed to break jail, he and Eastchurch sailed for England to present their case to the proprietors.

That was 1676, an ominous year in the southern colonies. In Virginia the popular uprising known as Bacon's Rebellion had been raging for months, only a few miles above Albemarle. For a time, the rebels ranged the colony unchecked, able to seize the capital city of Jamestown at will and force the frightened burgesses to vote whatever laws they, Bacon's men, desired. But then Bacon died, the rebellion fell apart, and Governor Sir William Berkeley was reestablished in authority. Enraged at the public humiliation he had suffered, Berkeley exacted a terrible revenge on whatever followers of Bacon he could find. One such rebel was William Drummond, Albemarle's first governor, appointed to that post by Berkeley himself.

When the former governor was brought before him, Berkeley made a low, sarcastic bow. "You are very welcome. I am more glad to see you than any man in Virginia. You shall be hanged in half an hour."

Drummond replied with dignity, "I expect no mercy from you, sir. I have followed the lead of my conscience."

He was condemned at one o'clock and hanged at four, and his wife and children were deprived of his property and banished to the wilderness. It is uncertain what happened to the dead rebel's body, but it may have been drawn and quartered and the parts posted up at various public spots as a warning to others.

Because of such ferocious revenge, sympathies in England, even King Charles's, tended to lie with the rebels. Tyrannical, self-serving, and out-of-control governors were out of style, and the Lords Proprietors naturally wanted no such trouble in their own colony. When Eastchurch and Miller denounced the antiproprietorial party for misrule and neglect of plantation duty, the eight appointed Eastchurch to the governorship and made Miller collector of customs.

Culpeper's Rebellion

The two Thomases started home triumphantly. On the way, their ship stopped at Nevis in the West Indies, and there Thomas Eastchurch met a wealthy lady who attracted him. In his new capacity as governor of Albemarle, he gave Thomas Miller a commission as interim governor and sent him on ahead. Eastchurch remained behind to court the lady.

Miller arrived early in 1677 and proceeded to take over the reins of government from his enemy John Jenkins. Then he got busy strengthening his personal position in the colony. He surrounded himself with a bodyguard of soldiers, arrested some of the most prominent men in the colony, and set a price on the heads of those he couldn't catch. In his other role as collector of customs, he set about collecting the hated plantation duty with vigor and ruthlessness. Within a few months, he had seized 817 hogsheads of "uncustomed" tobacco and collected over £2,000 in duty.

Naturally, Carolinians were wild to get rid of Interim Governor Miller.

Meanwhile, George Durant of Durant's Neck had not been idle. Sailing for England shortly after the two Thomases, he arrived to find that the Lords Proprietors had (not unnaturally) taken the side of the proprietorial party and appointed the pair to office.

"The people of Albemarle will revolt rather than be governed by Eastchurch," Durant warned them defiantly. But the Lords Proprietors were unimpressed, and he was sent away unsatisfied. There was nothing for the planter to do but return to Albemarle.

He sailed home on the *Carolina*, Zachariah Gillam master, arriving late in 1677. Gillam was a Bostonian with a penchant for "running" tobacco out of Carolina without the formality of paying customs duty. When the *Carolina* arrived in Pasquotank River, Miller had the skipper arrested for violating the customs laws. While he was at it, the interim-governor had Durant arrested as well.

Durant's allies in the antiproprietorial party decided that it was now or never for their cause. Surveyor-General John Culpeper and Valentine Byrd, Jenkins' "collector" of customs, gathered about forty citizens of Pasquotank precinct, armed them with guns taken from Gillam's ship, and surrounded Miller's house. He was seized, clapped in irons, and sent back to the jail from which he had escaped. Durant and Gillam were released. Then the rebels took possession of the tobacco Miller had collected and the records and revenues of the customs service.

After this bloodless coup, the rebels lost no time setting up their own government. On December 3, 1677, they published a proclamation stating that they had overthrown Miller because he was not the real governor appointed by the proprietors and that he was not conducting the office properly. They charged that Miller would not allow a free election and was cheating them out of their tobacco, and they demanded a free assembly in which to air their grievances.

While all this was going on, the surveyor-general instituted a search for the great seal of the colony, which was missing. Since documents promulgating decrees and laws were not considered legal until the official seal was affixed to them, it is certain that this search was prosecuted zealously. Culpeper finally found the seal hidden in a hogshead of tobacco. With this important device in their possession, the rebels were empowered—at least in their own minds—to call for new elections. They promptly did so.

When the votes were counted, Culpeper found himself the new governor. Just in time, too, for he had hardly been installed when word came that Thomas Eastchurch—the legitimate appointee of the Lords Proprietors— had arrived in Virginia with his West Indies bride.

On landing, Governor Eastchurch was told of the new situation in Carolina, and he hesitated to cross the border into the rebellious colony. Instead, he sent word to Culpeper and Durant to give up their government to his authority. By way of reply, the rebels sent a force of armed men to the Virginia border to prevent Eastchurch from entering. The distraught bridegroom asked the governor of Virginia (ironically named Thomas Culpeper, although no relation to the Carolina surveyor-general) for troops to install him in his office. Before action could be taken, Eastchurch died of a fever.

This left John Culpeper, Durant, Byrd, Jenkins, and their antiproprietory friends in control of the colony. But not for long. In 1679 Thomas Miller was loose. For the second time in his life, he had broken out of jail and fled to England.

High Treason

Like Durant before him, John Culpeper followed his enemy across the sea to England. But unlike Durant, the rebel leader had serious charges to answer.

By usurping Eastchurch's position as governor, Culpeper had merely offended the Lords Proprietors. But by seizing the confiscated tobacco and money from the customs office, he had defied the Crown. The case came under study by the Treasury, the Commissioners of the Customs, the Lords of Trade, and the Privy Council, who recommended that the unfortunate Culpeper be tried for high treason. His case appeared before King's Bench in 1680.

Things would have looked very black for Culpeper if the Privy Council had not also chosen to include the Lords Proprietors in its displeasure. Their lordships were ordered to submit a full account of the rebellion and present their charter to the council.

Afraid that the grant might be taken from them if it could be proved that they had mismanaged Carolina, the proprietors decided to play down the seriousness of the rebellion. Led by Ashley Cooper, now earl of Shaftesbury, they argued in Culpeper's favor: Since there had been no legal government in Carolina at the time of Culpeper's seizure of power (Governor Eastchurch having absented himself), he was guilty only of riot, not of rebellion. Moreover, Miller had acted without legal authority, had often been drunk, and by his arbitrary actions had put the people of Carolina in fear of their lives and property. John Culpeper was acquitted— a tremendous victory for the antiproprietorials.

Released, Culpeper returned to Carolina and devoted himself to surveying the by now ten-year-old settlement in the southern part of the colony, called Charleston. Miller, abandoned by the proprietors, disappeared from history. The proprietors debated among themselves how best to reestablish control over their colony.

There was no point in naming a governor from among the settlers already in Carolina, for whichever party he belonged to, proprietorial or antiproprietorial, the other party would oppose whatever he did. Someone from the outside was best, preferably one of themselves. Accordingly, they chose Seth Sothel.

By 1680, six of the eight original proprietors were dead, only Shaftesbury and Craven still surviving. Sothel had bought Lord Clarendon's share.

He was considered by the other proprietors "a sober and moderate man," and since he was—unlike his colleagues—perfectly willing to go live in Carolina himself, they named him governor. He managed also to obtain a commission as collector of customs, Miller's old job. The combination of these two offices in one person looked bad for the colony of Carolina.

Fortunately for the antiproprietorial party, the ship that was transporting Sothel to Carolina fell afoul of Barbary pirates, or "Turks," and he was carried captive to Algiers, where he was held for ransom. That meant Durant and his friends had four whole years in which to consolidate their power. After Culpeper's departure for England in 1679, the president of the council acted as governor for a while. At his death, the council named John Jenkins to the post once more, and soon "all things were in quyet and his Maj^tyes Customs quyetly paid by the people."

Then, in 1683, Sothel was ransomed from the pirates and came to Carolina to assume his postponed governorship. Peace departed from Albemarle.

A Colony Split in Two

Whatever "moderate" meant to the Lords Proprietors, it could not have referred to Seth Sothel's sense of restraint. For the new governor soon had men remembering Thomas Miller with nostalgia. Hotheaded and arrogant, Sothel seized estates illegally; confiscated cattle, slaves, and even pewter dishes from the people; and openly accepted bribes. When George Durant and another important planter, Thomas Pollock, protested this arbitrary and capricious behavior, Sothel blithely imprisoned them both and expropriated their estates. After six years of this oppression, the people of Carolina once more rebelled against their governor.

Perhaps they had heard of the Glorious Revolution of 1688, in which James II, successor to his brother Charles II, was deposed for attempting to institute arbitrary government in England, and replaced by his daughter Mary and her husband Prince William of Orange. Small ripples of similar upheaval had disturbed Massachusetts and Maryland, and perhaps it was backwash from all this that set Carolina settlers into motion.

Whatever triggered their actions, in May, 1689, a group of rebels, led by Thomas Pollock, who had managed to get out of Sothel's jail, marched to the governor's plantation on the Pasquotank River. Taking Sothel by surprise, they imprisoned him in a log jail and kept him there until he renounced the governorship, swearing "a strange oath," which has not been recorded.

The assembly tried him on thirteen charges, found him guilty, and banished him from the government. He lurked in Albemarle for a few months until word came that the proprietors, learning of the troubles in their colony, had suspended him pending an investigation.

Then, instead of returning to England, Sothel went south to Charleston, where he was granted one of only three seigniorships issued under the Fundamental Constitutions. He took up an estate on the Edisto River. Seignior Sothel was as much a troublemaker in Charleston as Governor Sothel had been in Albemarle, perhaps more. He had scarcely landed from his ship before he was seizing power from the acting governor (brother of another proprietor), imprisoning the colonial secretary after impounding his papers, confiscating property, extorting money, and intercepting men's letters from England. When the colonial court tried to depose him for "arbitrary, oppressive, irregular, illegal, and dangerous" actions, he defied it and the council. How dared the councilmen, he demanded, "sit theire without him theire head?" In this fashion, he continued to make trouble until his death in 1694.

This experience with Sothel seems to have brought the Lords Proprietors—that is, those who held proprietorships as purchasers or heirs of the original eight—to a decision. Their colony was too large to administer as a single unit. It was useless to try to govern Charleston on the Ashley River from Albemarle on the sound, and vice versa. The two settlements were three hundred miles apart as the crow flies and many miles farther by sea.

When they decided to name Philip Ludwell of Virginia as successor to the turbulent Seth Sothel, they ordered him to appoint a deputy governor for Carolina "north and east of Cape Feare." Henceforth there were to be two governorships and two colonies—South Carolina and North Carolina.

The history of the Old North State proper had begun.

CHAPTER TEN

Religion and Irreligion

Philip Ludwell, married to the widow of Sir William Berkeley, held the post of collector of customs in Virginia. That job kept him busy enough, and he preferred Virginia to either of the raw new settlements in Carolina. Besides, he knew all about settlers defying their governor, for he had done some defying of Virginia governors himself. So he remained where he was and governed from a distance—a system that worked, on the whole, rather well.

Only one incident marred Ludwell's governorship. In 1690, John Gibbs, a planter of Currituck precinct, issued a proclamation claiming that he and not the usurper Ludwell was the rightful governor of Carolina. He had been chosen by the council, he said, at the time it had banished Seth Sothel, and hence settlers owed obedience to him not to the imposter. If any supporter of Ludwell wanted to fight it out, he would duel with him hand-to-hand "as long as my Eyelids shall wagg."

Since no one took him up on this offer, Gibbs and some armed followers broke up the court at Currituck and made prisoners of two of the magistrates. North Carolinians gathered to the support of Ludwell, however, and Gibbs was forced to flee. Later in England, the Lords Proprietors rejected Gibbs and reaffirmed Ludwell's appointment to the governorship, but they ordered him to live in Charleston from then on.

The first deputy governor Ludwell named for North Carolina was Thomas Jarvis, one of the early settlers of Albemarle. Jarvis understood the settlers and their problems, and he was a man of good judgment, strong character, and administrative talent. He was followed in the deputy governorship by two other men who seem also to have been able administrators. The result was that the colony enjoyed over a decade of comparative peace.

Winking at the Law

Peace didn't necessarily mean that the residents of Rogues' Haven re-

Under Governor John Archdale, who was a Quaker himself, the Quakers of North Carolina prospered. But later, when the proprietors tried to establish the Church of England, they faced a struggle for their religious and political rights.

mained law-abiding subjects of King William and Queen Mary. They still continued to smuggle tobacco *out* of North Carolina in Yankee ships, after which it was smuggled *into* Scotland, Holland, and Ireland. The higher prices it brought overseas easily covered the costs of such roundabout shipping.

Then, too, men had discovered a use for the dangerous coast of the Outer Banks—raiding wrecks. As the Algonkian Indians, who had carried out this practice in early days, were driven back from the coast or otherwise elbowed out of the way, white people took over.

Salvaging wrecks is a very old practice, of course, dating to classical times. Much valuable material could be found aboard a cracked-up vessel. Even in the Dark Ages, English law was very strict about who had the right to strip which derelict. A wreck that was actually cast away (touching ground above water level) belonged to the Crown or to the person, usually feudal lord of the district, to whom such right had been specifically granted by the king. If the vessel still floated or was sunk below the surface, then it belonged to the Admiralty. The law also distinguished among flotsam (goods that have accidentally floated from the vessel through the action of the waves), jetsam (goods that have been deliberately jettisoned by the crew to save the ship), lagan (goods that have been tossed into the sea fastened to a buoy or sea anchor in hopes of recovering them later), and derelict (a vessel that has been abandoned by its crew).

Carolinians were unimpressed with such niceties. If they found a wrecked ship, it was theirs. In fact, they were inclined to take steps to keep it theirs. When an English ship, the *Hady*, was grounded between Roanoke and Currituck, people living nearby shot holes in her sides to prevent her being refloated.

Many Outer Banks people were not content to wait for what the storms of Cape Hatteras might bring them. They caused the wrecks themselves, often by trickery.

A favorite wrecker's device, it is said, was to hang a lighted lantern around the neck of a horse or mule and then walk the animal up and down the beach at night. A ship's crew, standing offshore and trying to find a safe channel in shoal water, would see only the lantern, bobbing gently as the horse walked. To a sailor's eye, a bobbing light suggested a ship's lantern, and the motion appeared to be that of a vessel smoothly under way. When the master ordered the ship's course changed to follow the light, he soon found himself aground and breaking up.

This practice is supposed to have given the area between Kitty Hawk and Oregon Inlet the name Nags Head.

Proposals for an Established Church

Ludwell was succeeded as governor by one John Smith, and he by John Archdale, a proprietor-by-purchase. Archdale was a Quaker, converted to the Society of Friends by George Fox himself, founder of the Society. There had never been much religious oppression in Albemarle, despite the fact that the Fundamental Constitutions did declare on paper that the Church of England was to be established there; the settlements were too remote and too poor for important churchmen to bother over them. Under Archdale this religious freedom was continued by design. But late in the century a move was underfoot among Virginians—the Church of England was solidly established in Virginia—to extend genuine establishment into the wilds of Rogues' Haven.

To modern ears this has the ominous ring of religious oppression. However, establishment did not always mean that dissenting religious bodies were persecuted—merely that all men were taxed for the support of the established church. Moreover, establishment brought other benefits to a colony than formal worship. In a day when social legislation and even organized charity were unknown, the church and its vestries were the chief means through which aid was funneled to the poor, the sick, and the orphaned. And in a rural colony, lacking the "town" system of New England, the parish provided a convenient local subdivision for governmental administration. To establish the Church of England in a colony meant to bring order.

Proponents of establishment knew it would be no easy task in North Carolina, however, for by the standards of staid Virginia, North Carolinians were a raffish, irreligious crew. As one Virginia missionary reported back, they fell roughly into four categories: 1) the "better sort," substantial planters like George Durant, Thomas Pollock, and others, few in number but Anglican by inclination and the natural leaders of the province; 2) Baptists (one of the earliest settlements in the American South of these staunch believers in freedom of worship), described as "some idle fellows, who preach and baptise through the country"; 3) Quakers, powerful enemies of all established religion; and 4) those with no religion at all, so depraved that they would have become Quakers except that they could not be bothered to live a moral life.

Anglican support, such as it was, lay chiefly in Chowan, the western-most precinct of Albemarle. Perquimans, next further east, was about half Anglican, half Dissenter (Quaker, Baptist, and Calvinist), and the eastern-most precinct, Currituck, was still chiefly a wild, mosquito-ridden swamp-land, where very few people lived and almost none professed religion at all. Pasquotank, in the center, was the chief center of Quaker strength.

The Quakers

Quakers had proselytized the colony early and often. The first Quaker settlers seem to have been a Mr. and Mrs. Henry Phillips, who moved to Albemarle from New England in the 1660's. In 1672, a Quaker preacher named William Edmundson visited them, and the Phillipses invited all their neighbors to come hear him speak. Many responded to the invitation, and the subsequent meeting is believed to be the first religious service ever held in North Carolina.

Edmundson was shocked that both men and women sat calmly smoking pipes as he preached the Inner Light, but his words must have struck a deep chord in these rough people, for "their hearts being reached by [the Lord's testimony], several of them were tendered and received the testimony." A few months after Edmundson's visit, George Fox himself arrived in the colony, traveling by foot and canoe all over Albemarle, and in his wake he also left many new converts to this religion of the common man.

Indeed, the Society of Friends is admirably suited to be a wilderness church. It requires no elaborate structure, no stained-glass windows, no steeple, no altar, no pulpit, no gold and silver communion vessels, no vestments, no choir, no long education in classical language and abstruse theology; in fact, no ministry. Members of the Society had only to meet on First Day in some crude shelter and open their hearts to one another.

The spread of Quakerism in North Carolina was very natural and steady, and in 1698 the first Yearly Meeting (the highest administrative unit in the Society) was formed in North Carolina. Nevertheless, some trying times were in store for the Friends.

The quarreling in North Carolina now took on a new hue. Instead of facing antiproprietorial colonists against the proprietorial party and the men sent over from England to govern, the colony was racked by dissensions among North Carolinians themselves. Realigned, it came to be the small planter, the backwoodsman, who supported the Quakers or the Baptists, against the large planters, who wanted an established church.

The Vestry Acts

Archdale was succeeded in the governorship by Sir Nathaniel Johnson, who appointed Henderson Walker, president of the provincial council, to be deputy governor of North Carolina. Walker was a stout Anglican, and it distressed him to see his colony "without priest or altar" or "worse." Under "worse" he filed Quakerism. The deputy governor urged the bishop of London—in whose see all North America was considered to belong—to send a qualified Anglican minister to North Carolina. When the bishop's choice turned out to be "ye monster of ye age," as one parishioner complained, Walker put the matter up to the assembly. The majority of members were Anglicans, and they voted the Vestry Act of 1701.

The act provided for the organization of vestries (the vestry was a body of men in each Anglican parish entrusted with managing the prosaic, day-to-day affairs of the church and its property), the laying out of parishes, the erection of churches, and the collection of a poll tax to support the Anglican clergy.

The Crown disallowed this act, chiefly on the grounds that it gave too much authority to the vestry and did not provide adequate salaries for the clergy. The proprietors' next deputy governor, Robert Daniel, was charged with obtaining a better Vestry Act from the assembly.

The Quakers and other Dissenters naturally resented such laws, which taxed them for the support of a religion and teachings to which they did not subscribe. They resolved to defeat this second act in the assembly. Deputy Governor Daniel resolved to see it pass.

Daniel, like Walker, was a fervent Anglican—and bigoted and brutal besides. He had an excellent weapon against the Quakers in a recent enactment of Parliament, which required every holder of public office to take an oath of allegiance to Queen Anne and the Protestant Succession. Oath taking was anathema to Quakers, and up to now authorities had been content with "affirmation"—a solemn declaration made under penalty of perjury.

When Quaker members arrived for the session, they were presented with the oath and ordered to swear. They refused and were denied a seat in the assembly. The second Vestry Act was then passed (1704), establishing the Church of England and English ecclesiastical laws in North Carolina. The assembly followed this up by making the oath taking even stricter than before.

Cary's Rebellion

The Calvinists and Baptists didn't mind about the oaths, but they disliked the rest of the Vestry Acts as much as the Quakers did. The three groups joined in a petition to Governor Johnson in Charleston, and he replaced Daniel with a South Carolina merchant named Thomas Cary.

Cary was no better than the man he had replaced. Tempestuous in character, enjoying disturbances, he was devoted heart and soul to one thing only—his own advancement. He enforced the oath vigorously, and not only barred Quakers from sitting in the assembly but induced that body to pass a law stipulating a fine of five pounds for anyone who accepted public office without taking an oath. Outraged at this, the Quakers sent a representative to London to present their case to the Lords Proprietors.

Archdale and one other proprietor were Quakers themselves, and it is probably owing to them that the Friends' case was heard so sympathetically. The representative returned to North Carolina in 1707 with the proprietors' orders that Cary was to be removed from office, the council was to elect a replacement, and free elections for the assembly were to be held.

When the messenger returned, Thomas Cary was away, visiting South Carolina, and his duties had evolved on William Glover, president of the colonial council. Since Glover was the man the council would probably have elected anyway, the Quakers accepted his acting governorship without objection. But, like Cary and Daniel before him, Glover also insisted upon the oath before admitting Quakers to the assembly.

The Quakers must have felt betrayed. They decided that Thomas Cary, after all, was the lesser of two evils. When he returned from Charleston, they did an about-face and joined the deposed governor in trying to depose his successor. Glover refused to be turned out of office, however, and the ensuing confusion is known as Cary's Rebellion.

Each would-be governor had his followers. Cary was supported by the Quakers and other Dissenters, who charged the Glover party with failure to maintain law and order (a favorite claim of people in times of political change) and with riding roughshod over the religious rights of the nonestablished churches. The Glover party derided this stand as the "Plebeian

Route." Glover himself was supported by the Anglicans, chief among them Thomas Pollock of anti-Seth Sothel fame, and he supported establishment of the church. Considering himself the legitimate choice of the proprietors, he excoriated Cary as "pretended president" of a "pretended council."

Before the two parties actually came to blows, they agreed to hold new elections to the assembly, hoping thereby to put the choice of governorship up to the voters. But since each side issued its own writs of election, two rival sets of assemblymen were voted into office. In October, 1708, they met under the same roof but sat in different rooms and continued the quarrel. Since Cary's followers were in the majority, however, the pro-establishment people at length gave up. Still maintaining that he was the lawful governor, Glover withdrew into Virginia.

The Queen's Cousin

For two years Thomas Cary was free to govern North Carolina as he pleased. All laws establishing the church were declared void, and a number

Governor Thomas Cary first opposed the Quakers, then championed them. When his replacement, Governor Edward Hyde, tried to reverse this trend, Cary led a revolt.
Finally, cornered by land and naval forces near Hyde's own house (shown here), Cary's followers abandoned him.

of Quakers were appointed to office without the oath. Then, in 1710, the proprietors, hoping to reestablish control of the colony, appointed Edward Hyde, a cousin of Queen Anne (her mother, the first wife of James II, had been Anne Hyde, daughter of the Lord Clarendon who was an original Lord Proprietor of Carolina), to the governorship of North Carolina.

At first the people's "awfull respect" for Governor Hyde's kinship to Anne brought peace between warring factions, and even Thomas Cary himself accepted the new state of affairs. But Hyde was tactless and appointed both William Glover, now back from Virginia, and Thomas Pollock to his council. When he called a new assembly in March, 1711, its members agreed that the various acts establishing the Church of England —the acts annulled by the Cary people during their two years in power— were legal.

This was too much for Thomas Cary. He called together his followers at his home, which was well armed, and defied the governor. He "brought together a gang of tramps and rioters," wrote an observer, "by means of promises . . . and good liquor, rum, and brandy, to which he treated the rabble . . . and they finally came to an open rebellion."

The assembly issued a formal indictment against Cary, charging him with high crimes. Governor Hyde collected forces to go against him. They met on June 30, 1711, near Pollock's house, where Cary was defeated and began to retreat. An appeal from Hyde to vigorous Governor Spotswood of Virginia brought aid in the form of a militia guard along the Virginia–North Carolina border and an armed vessel to patrol the sound. This show of force broke the already defeated insurgents' morale, and they began to slip away. When Cary and some of his lieutenants tried to flee into Virginia, they were captured and sent to England for trial.

The trial came to nothing. The proprietors, afraid of stirring up more trouble, dismissed the charges against Cary and sent him home to North Carolina, where he soon died quietly.

During all these years of troubles, disorder and confusion had reigned throughout the colony. Crops had been neglected so that men might fight or might serve in the assembly of their choice. Followers of one side or the other had marched here, assembled there, stirred up anarchy.

And as if all that turmoil were not enough, just as the political squabble was reaching its climax, the colony was beset with a furious onslaught from the one direction they did not expect it—from the long-suffering and frequently displaced Indians.

CHAPTER ELEVEN

The Tuscarora War

While the English settlers quarreled with one another over religion and politics, immigrants from other lands were entering North Carolina, in time to contribute heavily to its character and history. The earliest of these newcomers were French Calvinists, and in 1690 they settled near the Pamlico River—the first recorded settlement south of Albemarle Sound.

The Huguenots

Huguenots had been trickling out of France since 1628, the year their fortress, La Rochelle, fell after a famous siege. But from 1685 on, when Louis XIV revoked the French act of toleration called the Edict of Nantes, this trickle of emigrants swelled into a flood. Every Protestant country in Europe benefited from this windfall of skilled artisans, tradespeople, and scholars. Small numbers of them sailed to America, taking up residence in almost every colony then settled.

Huguenots flocked to South Carolina in larger numbers than elsewhere, and there was friction in early years between these Frenchmen and the English on the all-too-obvious grounds of their foreignness. But it was soon found that they held the political balance of power between the Anglican party and the Dissenters, and with both sides courting their favor, these differences of language and culture were soon settled amicably.

In 1707, a second group of Frenchmen entered North Carolina. They had settled originally in Virginia, but the land available there for grazing cattle had not been very good, and they had decided to move south. Led by their minister, Claude Philippe de Richebourg, they settled along the Neuse.

The Huguenot colonists in North Carolina made little splash. Wrote a British observer:

> They are much taken with the Pleasantness of that Country, and, indeed, are very industrious people. At present they made very good

Early explorers and surveyors of the Carolina interior sent home many accounts of the land, the natives, and the wildlife. Here are some illustrations from John Brickell's *The Natural History of North Carolina.*

Linnen-Cloth and Thread, and are very well vers'd in cultivating Hemp and Flax, of both which they raise very considerable Quantities; and design to try and Essay of the Grape, for making of Wine.

By 1700, the earliest of these communities, called Pamticoe, had come to the attention of the Albemarle authorities. This was not only the first settlement south of Albemarle, it was also the first that could be called a town, and the assembly decided to name it the colony's first official seat of government. (Until then, members of the assembly had met informally at one another's homes, and the governors had lived wherever it suited them.) Accordingly, they sent Surveyor-General John Lawson to lay out the new capital, which was formally incorporated March 8, 1705, and renamed Bath.

As the new capital of North Carolina, Bath was host to the sittings of the colonial assembly and home to the next five governors. In 1715, it became the official port of entry for the province. But in spite of these favors, Bath never did get very big. In its colonial heyday, it boasted twelve houses and a library with a small collection of books. The proprietors did nothing to encourage its growth, and no minister of the Gospel lingered there for long. As other parts of North Carolina were settled, Bath became more and more a backwater.

The Germans and the Swiss

Later still to seek asylum in North Carolina were a group of German and Swiss Protestants. In the first years of the eighteenth century, a blight struck the Rhine valley where most of them lived—caused partly by a series of wars, partly by extremely bad weather, and made worse by rumblings of distrust from neighboring Roman Catholic regions. Lured to England by a 1709 act of Parliament that offered citizenship to persecuted Protestants, these German-speaking emigrants found themselves stranded in London, without jobs and with dwindling supplies of money. An impoverished Swiss nobleman, Baron Christopher von Graffenried, discovered their plight, and since he was an adventurous man, he hit on the idea of taking them to Carolina. It was just possible that he might also, in the process, recoup his own lost fortune.

Von Graffenried had heard good reports of the colony from various sources. A Lutheran minister friend had written of the good relations between Indians and whites. One of the Lords Proprietors had discussed with him the beauty and riches of the Carolinas and had offered him a landgravate if he headed a major settlement in the region. And John Lawson, the man who had laid out Bath, heartily backed the project.

John Lawson, born in Scotland, had gone to America with an appointment as surveyor-general of North Carolina. Taking his job seriously, he had explored much of the Piedmont and the valleys of its rivers, had visited Indians in their villages, and had talked and listened to them extensively. The result was a book, *A New Voyage to Carolina*, which in time would come to be a major source for historians seeking information about early colonists and their Indian neighbors. Lawson went to London to see about getting it published.

Lawson and von Graffenried became friends. The Scotsman, who had built himself a plantation along the Neuse, agreed to accompany the first group of Germans to Carolina and help them get settled. Meanwhile, von Graffenried would wait for another assortment of emigrants from Bern, Switzerland, and would join Lawson later.

Lawson and his charges, 650 healthy, industrious, skilled young people, left England in January, 1710, in two ships. During the stormy voyage of thirteen weeks, a good half of the Germans died. Then, when at last they thankfully anchored in the James, a French privateer appeared—Queen Anne's War was then raging—and captured one vessel, stripping the passengers of everything they had brought with them. They set out overland —a terrible journey through swampy woodland—and finally reached the Chowan River. There Thomas Pollock (the wealthy antiproprietorial, pro-establishment man) furnished vessels so they might continue their voyage, and charged the earth for this service. But at long last the battered settlers arrived at the site of their new town.

Von Graffenried had assigned Lawson the job of picking a suitable place for this settlement, and accordingly he chose a spot between the Neuse and the Trent rivers. No preparations had been made for the settlers' reception, and although there were other settlers in the region, the loneliness of the Carolina wilderness soon began to prey on their nerves. Short of food, they had to trade their clothes for something to eat.

In September, 1710, von Graffenried arrived with 156 Swiss settlers. A natural leader, the baron immediately began to organize things. He sent to Pennsylvania for flour, had the land surveyed, forests cleared, houses built, and a water mill erected for grinding grain. He then gave John Lawson instructions for laying out a town:

> Since in America they do not like to live crowded, in order to enjoy a purer air, I accordingly ordered the streets to be very broad and the houses well separated one from the other. I marked three acres of land for each family. . . . I divided the village like a cross and in the middle I intended the church.

One street ran from Trent to Neuse, the other crossing it at right angles. When it was laid out as he had planned it, von Graffenried named the settlement for his home city in Switzerland: New Bern.

Under von Graffenried's authoritarian rule, the new town thrived and grew quickly. But it was barely a year old when disaster fell out of the blue.

Indian Grievances

New Bern had been built on land that belonged to the Iroquoian-speaking Tuscaroras. To these fierce, sophisticated people, this was the last of many straws.

Compared with Virginia and the New England colonies, North Carolina had had fairly peaceful relations with the original owners of the land. The Algonkians who had inhabited the shores of Albemarle had been shoved aside with little resistance, their lands seized often with cruel violence, and were forced back into swamplands. There they dwindled away by attrition, were carried off into slavery, or fell victim to smallpox or other diseases introduced by whites. But with the settlement of the Neuse and Pamlico valleys, whites had begun the same encroachment on the more powerful Tuscaroras.

In 1710, the Tuscaroras addressed a petition to the government of Pennsylvania. Perhaps they had heard of William Penn's fair dealings with the Susquehannocks, their kinsmen, for they asked to be allowed to migrate there. Their grievances against the Carolinians were many: Traders cheated them mercilessly. Their women and children could scarcely venture out of their palisaded villages to play or to fetch wood and water without being snatched up by kidnappers and carried off into slavery. If the men went hunting, the villages they left behind were subject to raids by marauding whites. If whites met Indian hunters in the woods, they thought nothing of killing them outright. There was the ever-present threat of disease, and now these newcomers had settled on their hunting grounds. Without having committed a single depredation against the whites, the Tuscaroras found themselves at bay.

Wrote Lawson, the expert, of the Tuscarora:

> They are really better to us than we have been to them, as they always freely give us of their victuals at their quarters, while we let them walk by our doors hungry, and do not often relieve them. We look upon them with disdain and scorn, and think them little better than beasts in human form; while with all our religion and education, we possess more moral deformities and vices than these people do.

However, Pennsylvania authorities did not want more Indians in their province—especially since their own Indians were disturbed at the thought of additional inhabitants with whom they would have to share hunting grounds—and they turned down this petition.

67

The Tuscaroras opened their 1711 rebellion by capturing Surveyor-General John Lawson, settler Christopher von Graffenried, and their Negro slave. In this drawing, by von Graffenried himself, the three captives are shown watching a war dance and threats to their lives. Only Lawson was actually slain.

Deprived of the only possible alternative to war, the desperate Tuscaroras allied themselves with a few dissident Algonkian tribes and turned on their tormentors.

It was September, 1711, when John Lawson set out up the Neuse River to do a little exploring. As surveyor-general of the colony, he wanted to find out how far upstream the river was navigable and how far off the mountains lay. He took along two friendly Indians, some Negro slaves, and von Graffenried. After they had journeyed a few days, they were set upon by a war party of some sixty Indians, who stripped them of their belongings and hustled them off to their village, called Catechna.

At first the Tuscaroras were inclined to release their captives unharmed, but after a night in the village a new group of tribesmen arrived and began to question the prisoners. During the questioning, Lawson got into a quarrel with one of these visiting Tuscaroras, and the angry Indians changed their minds. Both Lawson and von Graffenried were condemned to death.

They were taken out to an open space before a large fire, where the grizzled shaman made two white rings, with sand or flour, on the ground.

A wolf skin was laid down before the two victims, and a few feet farther off stood an Indian holding a knife in one hand and a tomahawk in the other—apparently the official executioner. He stood motionless while beyond the fire a circle of painted dancers pranced and howled. Behind the victims stood a line of armed warriors, and behind them the council of chiefs still deliberated.

At length the council changed their minds again and decided to spare one of the two intended victims. Ironically, because they mistook him for Governor Hyde, they spared von Graffenried. Hence, John Lawson, one of the few white men in the Carolinas who sympathized with their wrongs and respected their culture, was executed.

They tied the surveyor-general to a tree, stuck him "full of fine small splinters of torchwood, like hogs' bristles, and so set them gradually on fire." Probably, when he had suffered enough to satisfy them, they cut his throat with his own razor.

Massacre

The following day—von Graffenried was still their prisoner—the Tuscaroras revealed to the baron their plan to assault his colony and all other settlers south of Albemarle. By promising them to remain personally neutral throughout the conflict, he managed to make a private treaty with them, agreeing to give each chief a cloth jerkin, two bottles of powder, five hundred grains of small shot, and two bottles of rum. In return, they promised that New Bern itself would remain immune to attack. But von Graffenried could do nothing for those hapless settlers who lived in outlying regions.

On September 22, 1711, the warriors fanned out through the valleys of the Neuse, Trent, and Pamlico rivers, raiding isolated farms and plantations, sparing no one. An eyewitness described how one such family had been laid out by the mocking Indians:

> The old gentleman himself, after being shot, was laid on the house-floor, with a clean pillow under his head, his wife's clothes put upon his head, his stockings turned over his shoes, and his body covered all over with new linen. His wife was set upon her knees, and her hands lifted up as if she was at prayers, leaning against a chair in the chimney corner, and her coats [petticoats] turned up over her head. A son of his was laid out in the yard with a pillow laid under his head and a bunch of rosemary laid to his nose. A negro had his right hand cut off and left dead.

Another settler was found stretched out on his wife's grave. Women were impaled on stakes or had their unborn infants ripped out and hung on trees. Men coming to the aid of the victims found so many dead that they had no time to bury them all.

Over 130 whites were slain, twenty or thirty women and children taken prisoner. Over half the losses were sustained by the Swiss and Germans, although, true to their promise, the Tuscaroras left the village of New Bern alone. Many of the New Bernians, however, gathered at a fortified house outside of town and plotted to revenge themselves on the Indians. Even when the released von Graffenried arrived and explained to them the conditions under which he had obtained their immunity, they were not satisfied. About then a group of them captured a chieftain, and in thirst for revenge they roasted him alive. When word of this got back to the Tuscaroras, New Bern's immunity was over.

Their fury renewed, the Indians spread out over the entire region south of Albemarle, wiping out settlers, driving off cattle, burning houses. Albemarle itself was threatened, and the people there hastily fortified their plantations.

Governor Hyde wanted to act, but he knew that his Quaker-dominated assembly would refuse to vote militia supplies, so instead he appealed to Governor Spotswood of Virginia. Spotswood had some troops at his disposal, but he could not send them unless North Carolina agreed to supply them with provisions. But the growing season of 1711 had been very hot and dry, the harvest meager, and there was no food in North Carolina to spare. Hyde had to refuse this help and turn instead to his other neighbor.

This time he was not disappointed. The assembly of South Carolina, in a rare instance of concern for a fellow colony, appropriated £4,000 to send an expedition of friendly Indians under white leadership to the aid of its next-door sister. In command of this expedition was one Colonel John Barnwell.

Tuscarora Jack

Colonel Barnwell, who in time would be known as Tuscarora Jack for his exploits in this war, led out a force of thirty-three white men and five hundred Siouan-speaking Yamasee Indians. This little army made a prodigious march through three hundred miles of forest and swamp to the Neuse River, which they reached January 29, 1712. They turned toward Tuscarora country, where the Indians had hastily built forts. Barnwell attacked and took the strongest of these forts, seizing prisoners and allowing his men to take fifty-two scalps. The Tuscaroras and their allies abandoned their other forts and fled. Barnwell followed, destroying their villages, burning their stores of corn, and gathering up plunder that had been taken from whites. The South Carolinians reached Bath on February 10, where settlers wept tears of joy at sight of them.

Reinforced by some 150 North Carolina troops, Barnwell set out again at the end of February, his destination Catechna, the same village where von Graffenried had been held prisoner and Lawson burned. Since then the Tuscaroras had fortified it heavily, and from behind its bulwarks they turned a withering fire on their attackers. Some of the raw North Carolinians—" base, cowardly crew"—fled in panic, but the rest spent the first night digging entrenchments that threatened Catechna's boats and water supply. When the sun came up and the besieged Indians saw that their position had worsened sharply, some tried to flee, only to be driven back by Barnwell's fire. Over fifty white and Negro captives were in the fort. To put pressure on Barnwell's army, the Tuscaroras began to torture some of their prisoners.

Many of the North Carolinians who had stayed to fight had relatives among the Tuscarora prisoners. They begged Barnwell to make peace with the Indians, and at last he consented to parley with them. They agreed to release a dozen captives immediately and later to discuss a permanent peace, and Barnwell withdrew his men and marched to New Bern, arriving in mid-March.

But the Tuscaroras and their allies failed to appear at the appointed time, and Barnwell—reinforced with more North Carolinians and some Chowanoc (Algonkian) Indians—marched back to renew the assault. At the suggestion of Christopher von Graffenried, Barnwell took along some cannon, transporting them by horse litter, and grenades.* Arriving in the vicinity of Catechna, Barnwell built a triangular breastwork called Fort Barnwell, as a kind of base, and then moved forward against the Indian village.

But Catechna was well fortified and the Tuscaroras were desperate. Despite the heavy armaments of the whites, they held out. "For variety of action, salleys, attempts to be relieved from without," wrote Barnwell, this siege could not "be parallelled against Indians." After ten days of battering, of assaults, of attempts to burn the place, the whites were short of supplies. When the Tuscaroras offered to surrender under certain terms, Barnwell accepted. That was April 17, 1712.

The terms were harsh enough. The Tuscaroras and their allies had to surrender immediately all white and Negro captives and turn over certain of their war chiefs as hostages and others as prisoners. (One prisoner, considered a principal leader of the rising, was promptly hanged.) They were

---

* An eighteenth-century grenade was a round metal ball stuffed with projectiles, combustible material, and gunpowder, with a hole in the top. It looked like a pomegranate, hence its original name *granada* ("pomegranate" in Spanish). The grenadier thrust his lighted "match" (a piece of stiff cord dipped in sulfur) into the hole and ignited the combustible material. Then when a nice flame was flickering at the top, he threw the whole thing at the enemy—before, it was hoped, it exploded.

to give up all plunder and resign their corn supplies to the Yamasee. Henceforth, they were to stay away from all lands south of the Neuse—lands to be reserved to the Siouan tribes as hunting grounds—and confine themselves to a certain area north of the river. They were ordered to destroy the fort at Catechna and forbidden to build others, and they were to "come yearly to the Governor in March and pay Tribute." In return, all they received was the right to depart in peace.

For granting them this much, however, Tuscarora Jack Barnwell earned the indignation of the North Carolina assembly. The South Carolina colonel had lost five of his own horses and spent several hundred pounds of his own money in operating the expedition. But because he had not wiped out the Tuscaroras altogether, North Carolina authorities were miffed. When he asked for a grant of land in payment for his services, they refused. They even denied him a vote of thanks. Abandoning North Carolina in disgust, he headed for home—and was wounded en route. As retaliation, some of his followers seized and enslaved some Indians.

The Sixth Nation

This last action by the departing South Carolinians was enough to start up the whole business again. The Tuscaroras, considering that the whites had wantonly broken the peace, went back to war in the summer of 1712, "and the last troubles were worse than the first." To make matters more difficult yet for North Carolina, a yellow fever epidemic struck the colony that summer and carried off many settlers, including Governor Hyde, the Queen's cousin. Our old friend Thomas Pollock was named acting governor, and his first step was to take action in the Indian crisis. He appealed once more to South Carolina.

Despite North Carolina's shabby treatment of Colonel Barnwell, South Carolina again came to the aid of her northern neighbor. In November, 1712, Colonel James Moore, son of a former South Carolina governor, set out for the Neuse at the head of thirty-three whites and one thousand Indians. Moore joined forces with a sketchy force raised by Pollock. At Fort Nohoroco on Contentnea Creek (in modern Greene County) on March 25, 1713, the two sides fought a savage battle.

It was a "glorious victory" for the whites. Fifty-seven whites and their Indian allies were killed and eighty-two wounded. In return, the Tuscarora and their allies lost 950 men, women, and children killed and captured. Pollock reported, "Enemies Destroyed is as follows—Prisoners 392, Scolps 192, out of ye sd. fort—and att least 200 kill'd and Burnt in ye fort." Many captives were sold as slaves.

It was a decisive victory, and it put an end to Tuscarora power in North Carolina. The remnants of this once numerous people fled westward, and their allies took refuge in the swamp regions, whence Colonel Moore methodically weeded them out during the rest of 1713 and 1714. It was February 11, 1715, before the last of these allies—mostly Algonkian dissidents—signed a treaty agreeing to retire to a reservation near Lake Mattamuskeet.

Meanwhile, the scattered Tuscaroras sent a pathetic plea to their cousins in New York colony—the mighty Five Nations of the Iroquois: Take us in! We have nowhere else to turn. Give us refuge!

No one knows the exact date when the Five Nations made their decision, but by September, 1713, with the Oneida sponsoring their southern cousins, they were debating whether or not to accept them. By 1722 the decision was made, for in that year, at a council with the governor of New York colony, the Iroquois gave six shouts—five for the Five Nations, and a sixth for the Tuscarora, "lately seated between the Oneidas and the Onondagas." Henceforth the Iroquois would be known as the Six Nations.

Many whites were forced to leave North Carolina, too. De Richebourg, the Huguenot pastor, packed up many of his following and moved on south to the Santee River, in South Carolina. Some of the German and Swiss survivors at New Bern joined them, and Baron von Graffenried, forced to mortgage some of his hard-won property to pay for supplies he had bought from Thomas Pollock, finally lost heart. In the spring of 1713 he sailed for England, leaving his German-speaking settlers to get along as best they could.

Ironically, the Yamasee, who had served the whites of Carolina so nobly during the Tuscarora War, found themselves being cheated on its conclusion. They had been promised that prices for trade goods would be lower once the Tuscaroras were defeated. Instead, they were higher, and the outraged Indians plunged South Carolina into the Yamasee War. It was a disastrous time for everyone.

CHAPTER TWELVE

The Carefree Rogues

The Cary Rebellion, followed closely by the Tuscarora War, had left North Carolina a shambles. Many people had been killed, many others had fled to Virginia, and immigration had practically ceased. Houses and barns had been burned, livestock killed or carried away, fields laid to waste. The paper money that had been issued in 1712 and again in 1713, 1714, and 1715 had depreciated so much that it now passed for sterling at the rate of five to one. Since no crops had been planted, trade was at a standstill, and the public debt incurred by North Carolina to fight the Indian war was so great that Acting Governor Pollock estimated that it would take ten or twelve years to repay it. North Carolina seemed to have no future.

And yet, it was at this very low point in her history that the colony was born anew—by achieving her final and complete separation from South Carolina. Hitherto, the Lords Proprietors had appointed a governor for the Carolinas, to reside in Charleston, and a lieutenant governor for North Carolina, to reside in Albemarle. In 1712, however, it was decided that henceforth the two colonies should be distinct and altogether separate, and that North Carolina should have its own full-fledged governor. The first man named specifically to fill this new post, succeeding the dead Edward Hyde, was Charles Eden.

Eden was to bring an era of peace and good order and recovery to North Carolina, but his administration is remembered chiefly for pirates.

The Sea Robbers

North Carolina had long had an affinity for men who had gone "on the account." Accustomed to dealing with smugglers and evaders of the plantation duty, men of Albemarle could not see that it was so terrible for men to put to sea and seize a few unwary prizes—especially since, during the frequent European wars of the period, it was perfectly legal to obtain letters of marque (official papers authorizing a ship's captain to operate a private ship of war) and go aprivateering. Once the war was over, it was hard for such a man to slip back into dull and ordinary seafaring, and the natives of the Carolina shores sympathized with him. Besides, the men who took their small, shallow-draft vessels across the sounds, slipped through an inlet into the Atlantic, and fell on a passing merchantman, brought back much wealth into the impoverished colony—and goods that they sold far below the price of legal merchandise. Pirates were often the best asset an isolated community could boast.

Moreover, some proprietorial governors had also blinked at piracy. Seth Sothel and John Archdale were both believed to "favor illegal trade." No governor appears to have acted vigorously against pirates. In 1685, under orders from the Privy Council, the Lords Proprietors issued instructions that their colony must put a stop to "Treasons, Felonyes, Pyracyes, Robberyes, Murders, or Confederacyes," at sea or in any anchorage under their control. This evidently did not work well, for twelve years later the Board of Trade rapped the proprietors over the knuckles again. That was in 1697, and before there could be more complaints of North Carolina's easygoing attitudes, the long Queen Anne's War had been launched. From 1702 until 1713, colonial shipmasters might privateer to their heart's content.

But with the outbreak of peace in 1713, piracy became a problem once more—indeed, a worse one than ever. For in the later 1600's the Caribbean, where planters had become rich and respectable, no longer provided so many turn-a-blind-eye refuges for the sea robbers. As they looked about for new areas in which to locate, North Carolina seemed to offer excellent possibilities. There were the shallow sounds, for one thing—the big naval vessels could not follow a fleeing pirate sloop into shoal water. And communities were isolated—word of a man's misdeeds would take months to reach someone who might be willing to do something about them. In the four years between 1717 and 1721, nearly forty vessels were taken off the Carolina coast.

Among the Carolina pirates, there was Captain Edward Lowe of the *Fancy*, who liked to cut off his victims' ears or set them adrift in a mastless hulk. George Lowther of the *Happy Delivery* was such a coward that he would not attack any ship of near equal force; he ultimately committed suicide rather than submit to capture. Christopher Moody turned pirate before he was twenty-two and was hanged in London before he reached thirty. Captain Lewis of the *Morning Star* disliked English seamen and operated chiefly with a French and Negro crew, who eventually rose and murdered him. Charles Vane marauded up and down the Carolina coast for months before an expedition was sent out to capture him; it took the wrong man, and Vane escaped, only to be later hanged in Jamaica.

The "wrong man" whom the Carolinians took was Major Stede Bonnet himself, the gentleman pirate. A well-to-do planter of the West Indies, he is said to have gone to sea to escape a nagging wife. After a series of raids and piracies up and down the Atlantic coastline, Bonnet was seized and subsequently hanged at Charleston—but not before he had teamed up briefly with a man who was to become even more famous at this dangerous trade than Bonnet had been.

Blackbeard

Edward Drummond did not start out to be a pirate. He went to sea as an honest seaman from his native city of Bristol, England. During Queen Anne's War, he took service on a Jamaica privateer, capturing a number of French and Spanish ships for the glory of England. When the war ended in 1713, Drummond changed his name to Teach and simply continued in the business he knew best—capturing and plundering merchant vessels.

He signed on with a certain Captain Hornigold, who worked out of New Providence Island in the Bahamas. As they sailed up the coast of North America, Hornigold made Teach captain of one of the ships they had captured together. When they returned to the Bahamas, they learned that the king—it was George I by then—had offered a pardon to pirates if they would give up the trade and turn respectable. Hornigold was tired of pirating and accepted a pardon. But Teach was only getting started. He christened his new ship the *Queen Anne's Revenge*—"revenge" was a favorite name for a pirate vessel—and hoisted his own flag in her: black with a horned skeleton waving a spear at a large heart.

The Jolly Roger was originally a signal flag. It carried emblems of death —skull and crossbones, skeleton, arm and cutlass—and was intended to signify the horrible things that would happen to the victim if he did not instantly surrender. Later, however, it came to be displayed as an ensign, and every pirate liked to choose his own style. Captain Edward Lowe's *Fancy*, for instance, flew a black flag with a red skeleton.

No one knows exactly where the name "Jolly Roger" came from, but it may have originated in an old English word for the Devil—"Old Roger." Or since early pirate flags were red rather than black, it might originally have been "*joli rouge*," French for "pretty red." Some historians speculate that Roger was pronounced with a hard *g* and meant "rogue." Hence a man who displayed such a flag as Teach's advertised himself as a carefree rogue.

In any event, Edward Teach ran up his personal flag and set out to make a name for himself. Since an evil reputation helped to persuade victims to surrender without much resistance, Teach again changed his name, this time to Blackbeard. Before he went into action against a ship, he would plait his long, black, bushy beard into little pigtails and tie each one with a

Taking his name from his long, black, pigtailed beard, and bristling with pistols and cutlasses, Blackbeard made himself the terror of the North Carolina coast. A secret arrangement with the governor's secretary enabled him to raid colonial shipping unmolested.

colored ribbon. Then he would stick under his hat several slow-burning matches and light them so that wisps of smoke curled out around his head, adding to his frightening appearance.

From shoulder to waist across his chest he wore a bandolier in which he stuck three braces of pistols that were primed, cocked, and ready for instant firing. More pistols, daggers, and cutlasses were strapped around his waist with a belt. Thus he could fire repeatedly without having to stop to reload, and if the fight lasted long enough, he had the cutlasses to fall back on.

For a time Blackbeard cruised along the shores of Pamlico Sound, capturing and using several different ships. A despairing man wrote to a friend that Blackbeard "was of a most bloody disposition, and cruel to brutality; his name became a Terror; and some Governors being remiss to pursuing him, he almost put a stop to the trade of several . . . colonies."

Blackbeard's favorite refuge was Ocracoke Inlet in the Outer Banks. To this day an inlet near the village of Ocracoke is still called Teach's Hole. Here Blackbeard came to careen his ships. Like most pirates, he preferred a small ship to a large one, not only because it was better suited to the shallow North Carolina waters but because it was easier to careen—an important point with a vessel that did not dare frequent ports large enough to support ship-repair facilities.

Careening was necessary about three times a year, to rid the ship's hull of barnacles, which slowed down its speed under sail, and to tallow it as a protection against shipworm. To careen a vessel, the crew sailed her into shallow water until she ran aground. Then they shifted the cannon, cargo, and other heavy gear to one side, causing the ship to list, or lean steeply to one side. The pirates would then attach ropes and pulleys to a tree and pull the vessel still farther over until part of her bottom showed. That allowed them to scrape away the barnacles. When one side was clean, the ship was careened the other way, and the opposite side was cleaned. When the bottom had been scraped, the hull was treated with a daubing of tallow and sulfur.

While part of the crew careened the ship, other members made camp on the shore. They constructed a temporary fort by throwing up earthworks and bringing cannon from the ship to mount them on crude fortifications, preparing themselves in case of a surprise attack.

Governor Eden's Friend

Blackbeard decided to settle down in North Carolina. He and his crew had enough treasure to last for a while, and apparently he had heard that Governor Eden was friendly to pirates. On his way to the mainland, Blackbeard deliberately wrecked the *Queen Anne's Revenge* and marooned some of his men—no one knows why—on an uninhabited island without food, water, or ammunition, before completing the voyage in small boats. Landing, he swaggered up to the governor's home in Bath with about twenty of his men, and surrendered. Eden granted the king's pardon to all of them, and many people in the colony made them welcome. Blackbeard was soon boasting that he could be invited to any home in North Carolina.

The pirate bought a house at Plum Point, just across the creek from Governor Eden's home. Many people believe that an underground passage was dug from the governor's palace to the steep bank of the creek, through which the governor and his secretary, Tobias Knight, received their share of Blackbeard's plunder.

According to a popular legend, Blackbeard wanted to marry Governor Eden's daughter, but she was in love with another man. Infuriated at being rejected, the pirate ordered his men to seize his rival, and he put out to sea with the unfortunate suitor aboard. There he ordered that one of the prisoner's hands be cut off and that he be thrown into the sea. Blackbeard sent the hand to Miss Eden in a silver casket. She still refused to marry him, however, and soon after died.

Although Miss Eden may or may not have spurned him, Blackbeard's lavish display of silks, gold, and jewels so dazzled one sixteen-year-old girl that she consented to marry him. Rumors said that Blackbeard already had twelve wives living—or dead, murdered by their brutal husband—in various ports in the West Indies, but this did not stop the governor from attending the wedding.

The bride, whose name is not recorded, soon regretted her decision. Blackbeard treated her with such cruelty that even the members of his crew protested.

For a few months the pirates lived a life of merrymaking. They entertained on a lavish scale and made friends with the planters in the neighborhood by giving them rum and sugar. But with such expenses and no new revenue coming in, even Blackbeard's fortune ran out. There was nothing to do but go back to pirating. He opened his new career in a new ship, named the *Adventure*, by robbing the vessels of neighbors who had been his guests. No one dared identify him as the pirate because he was a friend of the governor.

This small-time piracy was not enough, however. Blackbeard sent word to old members of his crew to rejoin him, and he began to make ready for sea again. When anyone asked where he was going, he replied that he was making a trading expedition to the West Indies. Soon the pirates sailed down the river to the open sea. A few weeks later the *Adventure* returned to Bath with a big French ship captive.

Blackbeard told the governor that he found the ship without any crew on it, drifting at sea. Governor Eden convened a court, at which Tobias Knight sat as the judge. The ship was condemned, and the pirates were allowed to sell the cargo of sugar, spices, and rum. Afraid that someone might recognize the vessel, Blackbeard said that it was too leaky to be seaworthy, towed it up the river from Bath, and set it afire. What did not burn was sunk. It was said in Bath that Governor Eden received sixty hogsheads of sugar and Tobias Knight twenty as their share of the loot.

Secure in his friendship with the governor, Blackbeard attacked any ship that crossed his path. The many rivers along the coast of North Carolina and Virginia were his private domain. He demanded provisions from the plantations along the banks of the streams, sometimes trading for them but often taking them by force. Every captain along the coast of North Carolina and Virginia wondered, as he took his ship out of port, if he would be able to slip by the pirates.

Battle to the Death

In 1717, Governor Alexander Spotswood of Virginia reported that sea traffic was practically at a standstill because of the pirates off the capes. For six weeks not a ship dared to leave Virginia ports. Spotswood decided that something must be done. Because Blackbeard had accepted the king's pardon, he could not legally be called a pirate, unless actual evidence of piracy could be found. When William Howard, who had been quartermaster (petty officer in charge of the helm) for Blackbeard, was captured in Virginia, his testimony corroborated what Spotswood already believed—namely, that Blackbeard and his crew, after accepting the king's pardon, had returned to piracy.

Governor Spotswood received word that Blackbeard had entered Ocracoke Inlet with another prize. It was also rumored that the pirate planned to fortify Ocracoke and make it a refuge for pirates.

The Outer Banks were a long way from Virginia and thus well outside Spotswood's range of authority, but this energetic and able governor was not to be stopped by a technicality. He decided to send an expedition to capture Blackbeard. But he needed to keep the business secret, for far too many colonists—Virginians among them—were accustomed to cooperating with freebooters. Consequently, he could not ask the assembly for funds. With money from his own pocket, he hired two small, fast sloops and two pilots familiar with the shoal waters of Ocracoke Inlet. Wanting trained fighting men to crew the sloops, he chose fifty-five sailors from two British warships in the harbor. Lieutenant Robert Maynard was put in command of the *Ranger*, and Captain Ellis Brand was given overall command of the expedition.

On November 17, 1718, the two sloops quietly sailed out of Chesapeake Bay and set a course for Ocracoke Inlet. Four days later, having left Captain Brand at Bath to gather evidence, the *Ranger* and the smaller sloop sailed into the inlet, where they saw the *Adventure* anchored in open water. Maynard dropped anchor to wait until dawn before he attacked.

Blackbeard regarded the approach of the two ships with cool bravado. He must have known they were after him, but to demonstrate that he feared nothing, he spent a good part of the night drinking with the captain of a merchant ship. Maynard, on the other hand, spent the night preparing for the next day's battle.

At sunup, Lieutenant Maynard put small boats overboard with instructions for them to take soundings between the ships, so there would be no risk of running aground. When Blackbeard saw they were within range of the *Adventure*, he ordered a round of shot to be fired, and the rowboats scurried back to the safety of the sloops. Next Maynard ordered the small sloop to close in on the *Adventure* and board. As the *Ranger* approached the pirate ship, she stuck on a sandbar, and the crew had to throw ballast overboard before she was light enough to float off.

The small sloop also ran aground, and no matter how the crew tried, they could not get her loose. Blackbeard ran up the Jolly Roger on the *Adventure* and went into action. He fired a broadside at the stranded small sloop, killing the commanding officer and several of the crew. Turning quickly, he fired at the *Ranger*. The *Ranger* carried no cannon, and the range was too long for muskets. Maynard had to get in close to the pirate ship before the cannon blasted his sloop out of the water.

The wind died down, and Maynard ordered the heavy oars to be manned. Blackbeard fired another broadside right into the rowers, killing some and badly wounding others. Maynard ordered his men to go down into the hold but to keep their pistols primed and cutlasses ready for instant action. Only Maynard, the helmsman, and a few men remained on deck.

Blackbeard, thinking that he had already won the fight, brought the *Adventure* alongside the *Ranger* to board it. The pirates threw grenades made of boxes filled with powder, small shot, and scrap iron onto the deck of the *Ranger*. Since most of the men were below, this did little damage. Through the smoke only a few men could be seen running about on the deck. Blackbeard shouted to his men to board.

When the pirates climbed over the gunwales, Maynard's men swarmed up from the hold. Pistol shots and the clatter of clashing cutlasses mingled with the cries of dying and wounded men. Suddenly, Maynard met Blackbeard face to face. Both men fired their pistols almost point-blank, but Blackbeard missed. The ball from Maynard's pistol plowed into Blackbeard's body—but scarcely slowed him down. The two men drew their cutlasses, and with a powerful sweep, Blackbeard snapped Maynard's sword in two. Then, staggering slightly, the pirate raised his sword for the death blow. At that moment one of Maynard's men rushed in with his sword and slashed Blackbeard's throat as the pirate's sword swung down and cut Maynard across the knuckles.

Even with his throat cut and a pistol ball through his body, the incredible Blackbeard fought on. He pulled a pistol from his belt. But as he cocked it, he finally toppled over, dead.

With more than half of the *Adventure*'s crew killed and their leader dead, the remaining pirates surrendered. Ten men of Maynard's crew were killed and twenty-four were wounded.

When Blackbeard's body was searched, a letter was found in his pocket. It began "My Friend," and was signed "T. Knight." It warned the pirate that Governor Spotswood was sending Maynard to fight him.

A Pirate's Accomplices

Maynard cut Blackbeard's head from his body and hung it from the bowsprit of the *Ranger*, then set sail for Bath. In that capital, Captain Brand had also been busy. With the help of two members of the local militia, he had discovered that Tobias Knight's barn was filled with pirate loot. When Knight was accused by Brand, at first he protested that he did not know what Brand was talking about. But when he was shown Blackbeard's account book, which listed the goods given to him, the secretary changed his mind. He had only been storing the goods in his barn, he said —storing them for Blackbeard, who he thought was a respectable tradesman. Brand ordered that all the goods be put aboard the ships under his command, and with Blackbeard's head still dangling from the bowsprit of the *Ranger*, he and Maynard set sail for Virginia.

Governor Eden soon discovered that the pirate goods had been taken away. He protested vigorously to Governor Spotswood, saying that Spotswood had no right to invade North Carolina waters and demanding that the Virginia governor return the captured pirates to North Carolina for trial. When Spotswood sent him a copy of William Howard's testimony,

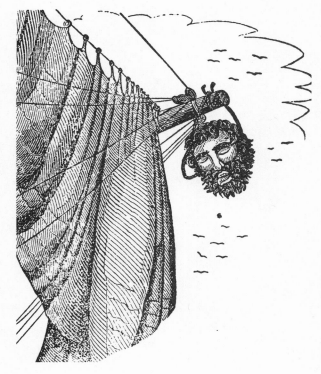

As proof of his victory, naval Lieutenant Maynard hung the pirate's head from his bowsprit and set sail for Bath to present evidence of collusion to the North Carolina authorities. Secretary Tobias Knight was acquitted despite ample proof of his guilt.

however, Eden had to back down. Public opinion even forced him to bring his secretary, Tobias Knight, to trial.

On May 27, 1719, the secretary appeared before the governor's council. The handwriting of his letter to Blackbeard was compared with other documents he had written and was found to be the same. However, Knight still denied that he or Governor Eden had had anything to do with Blackbeard. The members of the council all sided with him and said that Knight was a good and faithful officer. They declared that the evidence brought against him was false, and handed down a verdict of not guilty.

Blackbeard's death brought the beginning of the end to piracy on the coast of North Carolina, but the legend of Blackbeard spread throughout the world.

In Boston, a twelve-year-old printer, apprenticed to his brother, was inspired by Blackbeard's story to retell it in verse, under the title "Sailor's Song on the Taking of Teach the Pirate."

> "Then each man to his gun,
> For the work must be done
> With cutlass, sword and pistol.
> And when we no longer can strike a blow,
> Then fire the magazine, boys, and up we go!
> It is better to swim in the sea below
> Than to hang in the air and feel the crow,"
> Said jolly Ned Teach of Bristol.

Not exactly Shakespeare, but even Benjamin Franklin had to start somewhere. As for North Carolina, the colony was better off for having gotten rid of "jolly Ned Teach of Bristol."

CHAPTER THIRTEEN

A Royal Colony

The fertile valley of the Cape Fear River had remained unsettled since the Barbadians left it in 1667. During the heyday of piracy along the Carolina coast, it had been a favorite careening place for freebooters. And the Siouan Indians of South Carolina claimed it as their hunting ground. But early in the 1720's, with the suppression of piracy, a few families from Albemarle began to move south into this region.

When George Burrington succeeded Charles Eden as governor in 1724, settlement of the Cape Fear valley was speeded up. Governor Burrington had explored the region himself, and he was convinced that North Carolina needed to establish claim to it. Not only was it a promising area for opening up, but if North Carolina didn't hurry, South Carolina would forestall her. Accordingly, some large grants were made to important landowners—two of them Maurice and Roger Moore, brothers of Colonel James Moore who had led the second South Carolina expedition against the Tuscarora Indians—and a town named Brunswick was laid out on the west bank of the river. Within four years of its founding, this little hamlet became the seat of newly set up New Hanover County.

Seven years after the founding of Brunswick, another settlement was made about twenty miles farther up the Cape Fear River. A few English freeholders built some log shacks on a bluff near where the two main branches of the river join. They called their settlement New Liverpool. Two more groups of settlers moved nearby, naming their villages New Carthage and New Town, or Newton. In 1739, the then governor of the colony decided that this trio of settlements should be one town, and he accordingly renamed it Wilmington in honor of the Lord Privy Seal, Spencer Compton, earl of Wilmington. (That same year, in the colony of Delaware, another town was being renamed for this same English politician.)

Although situated thirty miles from the sea, Wilmington was to become

This exhibit at the North Carolina Museum of History shows the colony's two chief products—naval stores and tobacco. Naval stores were obtained from the pine trees that abound in the region. The trees were slashed and the liquid allowed to flow into containers. Its composition was then broken down by distillation into turpentine, creosote, resin, and wood tar.

North Carolina's only major seaport. The river's mouth was guarded by treacherous Frying Pan Shoals, and its estuary was likewise too shallow and navigation too difficult to manage large ships. Nevertheless, Wilmington was to be the major outlet for a new product of the colony: naval stores—tar, resin, turpentine, lumber, potash, barrel staves, and other fruits of North Carolina's great pine forests. In time the state would be as famous for this as for her tobacco.*

The Carolinas Return to the Crown

Meanwhile, the Lords Proprietors had been under great pressure from the Crown to surrender their grant. Both colonies had been mismanaged, the government felt. The Navigation Acts had gone unforced, plantation duty uncollected, the king's customs openly flouted, piracy allowed to

* The nickname "Tarheel State," however, is postcolonial, being attributed to General Robert E. Lee. Lee said that his North Carolina soldiers stuck to their work as though their heels were gummed with their native tar: "God bless the tar-heel boys!" Earlier, North Carolina was simply "The Old North State."

flourish. Even the Church of England was established only on paper. The proprietors had done little or nothing to fulfill the ostensible purposes of the charter—to spread Christianity, to enlarge the Empire, to encourage commerce.

The present holders of the eight proprietorships were discouraged anyway. Their vast territory had brought them little profit. Their idealistic Fundamental Constitutions had failed miserably. Their governors had been thrown out of office, driven into exile; ministers appointed to parishes in the colony had been hooted from their pulpits. What good were they deriving from their hold over this turbulent, vulgar, impossible colony?

At last, seven of the eight gave in and agreed to sell their shares of Carolina to the Crown for £2,500 apiece, plus a lump sum to satisfy claims to quitrents. The eighth, a grandson of Sir George Carteret, was John Carteret, earl of Granville, who insisted on retaining his share. A portion of the middle of North Carolina was accordingly marked off as rightly his, and on July 25, 1729, the balance of both North and South Carolina became royal colonies.*

The first royal governor—succeeding the last proprietorial, Sir Richard Everard—was George Burrington. In this, his second term in North Carolina, Burrington's chief concern was the border between his colony and South Carolina. (An earlier squabble with Virginia over the northern border had been slowly and painfully settled before the colony became royal.) Some South Carolinians claimed the Cape Fear as the natural boundary. North Carolinians naturally preferred the Pee Dee (a good thirty-five miles inside modern South Carolina).

In London, before he sailed for his new post, Burrington had agreed with the governor of South Carolina and the Board of Trade that the boundary should lie parallel to the Cape Fear and thirty miles southwest of it. Once he reached North Carolina, however, Burrington changed his mind and refused to have the line surveyed. The Pee Dee was a natural boundary, he said—that should be used.

Knowing that territory usually went to the colony that had the most settlers there, he encouraged emigration to the Cape Fear region. Then, with some Indians as guides, he personally spent seven weeks laying out a road that would connect the Cape Fear with Albemarle.

Burrington, an irascible, quarrelsome man, was recalled, but his successor, Gabriel Johnston, proved equally determined to promote settlement of the

* That portion was held by Granville and his heirs until 1776, when it reverted to the state of North Carolina at the time of independence. By then the tract, originally of very little worth, had become populous and immensely valuable, and the family sued to recover possession. But the newly established American courts ruled against them.

Cape Fear valley. Johnston moved to Wilmington (he was the man who renamed it), and since the courts and council followed him, that town automatically became the colonial capital.

At last, in 1735, he and the governor of South Carolina agreed to appoint commissioners to make a survey. It took six weeks of arguing, but they finally decided that the line should start "at the Sea, thirty miles from the West side of the mouth of the Cape Fear River, to run on a northwest course to the thirty-fifth parallel of north latitude, and from thence due east to the South Seas." (Most colonies claimed, grandiosely, to run all the way to "the South Seas"—that is, to the Pacific.)

This line was actually run by the commissioners from the sea to the Little Pee Dee, about one hundred miles. But the survey did not settle the dispute, for each colony continued to claim land—and collect taxes from its owners—on both sides of this border. New surveys were run in 1764 and 1772, but the two colonies had long been states of the new republic before a firm boundary was established and accepted.

Highland Scots

In the 1730's people of Welsh extraction began to drift into southern North Carolina, taking up land along the Northeast Cape Fear. These were seasoned people, mostly from Pennsylvania and Delaware, but they retained their ethnic identity strongly enough for their region to be named the Welsh Tract. At about the same time, a group of "poor Protestant families" from Ireland settled in the same general area as the Welsh Tract. Then the first of the Highland Scots appeared in North Carolina.

To understand Scotland's contribution to the settlement of North Carolina, something of that small, barren, remote, bleak country itself must be understood. Scotland had two populations really, and they were quite distinct from one another—unlike the popular American image of a Scotsman, which is that of a Lowlander (penny pincher) in Highland garb (bonnet and kilt).

The Lowlands were occupied by a people who spoke "broad Scots" (the language of Robert Burns), a dialect of English that contains many Teutonic words. They were probably of Norse origin, and were tough, disputatious, poor, equalitarian—laird and tenant spoke as equals, man to man—and largely Presbyterian. (The Church of Scotland is Presbyterian.) Education was more broadly based in the Scottish Lowlands than anywhere in Europe, and this coupled with poverty led many Scots to emigrate to America as teachers. We probably got our term "high school" from them.

Being staunchly Protestant, the Lowlanders tended to side with the anti-establishment people and to support the Crown against Jacobite revolutionaries—that is, risings in favor of the Roman Catholic Stuart family. This sturdy Protestantism is what made the English establish a strong settlement of them in Ulster, northern Ireland, in 1609. Called the Plantation of Ulster, this scheme eventually began to crumple under English economic restrictions on all of Ireland, and by 1700 these transplanted Lowlanders—known in America as the Scotch-Irish—had begun to stream across the sea to the colonies.

They went to Pennsylvania first, spreading out through the backcountry, where they took naturally to life on the frontier. Then, as the Susquehanna Valley filled up, they turned south to Maryland and Virginia. In time they would reach North Carolina by the back door—the Piedmont and the mountains.

The people of the Scottish Highlands were quite different. Celtic by race, most of them spoke no English at all. Erse, a form of Gaelic, was their language, and the majority were illiterate in it. Tribalism still prevailed in the Highlands, where hereditary chieftains ruled extended families called clans (from *clann*, meaning "offspring"). What religion they knew was as often Anglican or Roman Catholic as Presbyterian, and by

The poorer Gaelic-speaking Highlander often had a single garment to his name—the belted plaid, which formed both kilt and shawl. Blue bonnet and deerhide brogues completed this scanty costume.

trade they were either tenant farmers on a very small scale or shepherds. Conservative by nature, they liked authoritarianism and romantic lost causes, and they supported the Stuart monarchy.

The poorest of these Highland clansmen often had only one garment to his name—the belted plaid. (In Scots parlance, "plaid" means a garment, not a design.) A flat piece of woolen cloth five or six feet long, the plaid was worn wrapped around the body and held in place with a belt, the lower half forming the kilt, the upper half a kind of shawl. This same belt might also support a cowhide purse to carry a bit of oatmeal and perhaps a griddle to cook it on, and a long broadsword called a claymore (from *claidheamh mor*, meaning "great sword"). The plaid would be of tartan, but its wearer would choose any pattern that suited his fancy; if he were rich enough, he might even wear two different setts (patterns of weave) at the same time. "Clan tartans" as such were only just beginning to come into fashion in the eighteenth century.

On his feet, this man would wear crude shoes of untanned deerhide, often with the hair still on, called brogues (from *broc*, meaning "foot covering"—it has nothing to do with the word for an Irish or Scots accent). On his head, if he could afford such an extra, he wore a small tam-o'-shanter called a bonnet. This was always blue in color, and for gaiety or pride, its owner might decorate it with an eagle's feather or a sprig of greenery representing his clan badge.

This man's chieftain, to whom he was blindly loyal and devoted, lived somewhat better than a common clansman. No one was rich in Scotland, but rents paid by tenants allowed a clan chieftain to maintain the life style of a gentleman. Sons were educated, often in France, and manners might be elegant. The chief would deck himself in tartan, too, for this complicated weave was Scotland's national cloth, worn even by Lowlanders. The chief might even wear the belted plaid; but if so, he clothed his upper body stylishly in shirt and coat and draped the shawl part of the plaid around his waist or caught it up in a brooch at one shoulder. Or he might wear a plain jacket and tartan trews (from *triubhas*, meaning "trousers"), leg coverings snug enough to be considered tights. Or he might simply sport a fashionably cut suit all of tartan. What he would *not* wear is the modern Scots costume of neatly pleated kilt and separate plaid—that is largely a nineteenth-century invention.

If this elegantly mannered, stylishly dressed clan chief wished to go to war, he summoned his tenants and gillies (servants, from *gille*, meaning "boy"), and they buckled on their claymores, filled their purses with oatmeal, and went with him. If they did not, he burned down their huts over their heads.

Like many primitive cultures, the clan system worked only as long as

Highland gentlemen also wore the belted plaid, but they set it off with sophisticated upper garments and elegant buckled shoes. The favorite arm of the Highlander was the fearsome claymore, or broadsword.

conditions remained stable. Change made broad cracks in it, and in the 1730's, overpopulation began to plague the Highlands. Many of the chiefs, finding sheep raising more profitable than agriculture, were turning out their tenants and transforming cropland into pasture. Where were the dispossessed to go?

Three men in Carolina had a suggestion: the valley of the Cape Fear River. The men, themselves Highlanders, were James Innes, Hugh Campbell, and William Forbes, and between them they had been granted nearly three thousand acres in what is now Bladen County. They sparked the first immigration from the Highlands of Scotland to North Carolina.

Governor Gabriel Johnston, another Scot, encouraged such immigration also by writing home glowing accounts of the opportunities available to new settlers. Soon the Highlands had begun to stir, singing in Gaelic, "*Dod a ah'iarrhuidh an fhortain do North Carolina*"—"Going to seek a fortune in North Carolina." The Scotch-Irish settled in many different colonies, but the Highlanders came almost exclusively to North Carolina.

In 1740, a group of 350 arrived at once, in other years they came in lesser numbers—fifteen to twenty thousand in all. In the aftermath of the Rising of 1745, in which the clans supported the attempt of Prince Charles Stuart to seize the throne of England for his father, emigration soared. The English government, which had had a good fright, overreacted and sent troops sweeping ruthlessly through the Highlands, exacting a grim revenge. Houses were burned and families driven out to the hills. Highland dress was forbidden. Tenants were forced to pay rents to new "owners" of their chief's land (a number of them simply took food from their children's mouths and paid a double rent, sending the second to their chief in exile). To escape this dismal scene, many were happy to leave their native glens for the warmer, more hospitable forests of North Carolina.

The hardships of the wilderness meant little to these Highlanders. At home they had lived in stone huts floored with dirt, roofed with thatch, a hole in the roof to let out the smoke. Here a sunny climate replaced the dank mists of their homeland, and plentiful forests permitted a man to build a good-size house with a chimney, puncheon floor, board siding, and separate kitchen connected to the main house with a raised wooden walkway. This dwelling could be easily furnished with as much furniture as the owner needed and could fashion with simple tools. Many such dwellings were substantial buildings and even sported windows, a great luxury to the Highlanders.

Some Highlanders farmed, but most engaged in the manufacture of turpentine or other naval stores. Gradually they gave up their plaids, packed away their claymores, learned to live like the other settlers. But their language hung on. As late as 1828, travelers reported that there was a twenty-mile-wide district, centered on the Highland settlement at Cross Creek (modern Fayetteville), where only Gaelic was spoken. No other colony could make such a claim.

CHAPTER FOURTEEN

A Settled Way of Life

By now North Carolina was beginning to lose its raffish character and take on the appearance of a settled, stable colony. Her boundaries firmed up, she was no longer the complaisant refuge for her neighbor's runaway servants. Indeed, she had her own indentured servants—some of them convicts or debtors, sentenced to serve seven years in the colonies; some volunteers, indentured for four years to pay for their passage over; some orphans, sent overseas to be servants until they came of age. Usually these people were sold right off the ship by the captain who had transported them to the New World. Or an entrepreneur, called a soul driver, might buy them up on speculation and march them through the country, selling one here and another there like an itinerant peddler.

At the end of their term of service, they had to have "freedom dues." In early days, this meant fifty acres of land. Later it was changed to corn and clothes, later still to money. Some did not wait until they had worked out their terms and simply fled—as earlier North Carolinians had fled from their Virginia masters—usually to the backcountry.

However they achieved their freedom, it was not difficult for them to live thereafter. Land was plentiful and still fertile. If they did not want to bother with a cash crop—that is, tobacco—they could still subsist by raising corn and a few pigs, soon to become the traditional rural American meal, "hog and hominy."

A small vegetable garden furnished collard, mustard, and turnip greens; greens seasoned with fatback made a good meal, the "pot likker" soaked up with cornbread. Knives, forks, and spoons were made of wood or bone, and dishes and bowls were also wooden. A piece of real "chiny" was not used to eat from but was displayed as an ornament on the shelf of the cupboard or larder.

Earning a living took up very little of their time, and the rest, as a visitor observed, "is spent in sauntering thro' the woods with a gun or sitting under a rustick shade, drinking New England rum made into grog, the most shocking liquor you can imagine." This way of life so suited some of these people that they would move rather than give it up. When civilization threatened to come too close, or there seemed to be too much order and too many officials moving into their county, they would pack up their few belongings and head a few miles farther west. Crude, ignorant, lazy, they nevertheless led the way toward western expansion.

Blacks, Slave and Free

Black slaves had also come to North Carolina, the first ones arriving some time before 1700. A slave was far more expensive to buy than an indentured servant, so slave owning was a rich man's luxury. North Carolina still had a few wealthy planters and consequently comparatively few slaves. The slave population never got higher than 25 percent of the free—compared to 50 percent for a time in Virginia and 60 percent in rice-growing South Carolina.

In early days, black servants were considered to be in a condition similar to that of white bond servants—that is, they were freed after a set period of time. A master might manumit (free) one of his slaves as a reward for faithful service, or bequeath freedom in his will (although this was not likely for a man with many dependents, for slaves were a valuable form of property, and manumission would disinherit the heirs). As early as 1701, freed Negroes were voting in North Carolina elections, although later legislation insisted that freedmen leave the colony within six months. Later, slavery came to be considered a lifetime condition—unless individual good fortune happened to set a man free.

The slave had no legal rights. He could not testify against a white man, nor could he be tried in the same court as a free man. Slaves could not travel without passes from their owners, could possess no firearms, and were not allowed to meet or even communicate with one another at night. A sensible slave owner treated his blacks with consideration and concern, but no law forced a white man to be sensible. However, many penalties were exacted from blacks who stepped out of line. A 1741 law declared that any runaway slave had to wear an iron collar, stamped "P.G." for "Public Goal." Dr. John Brickell, an Edenton physician, wrote in 1731 that he had seen "Negroes whipped until large pieces of skin were hanging down their backs."

Many owners, believing it perfectly acceptable to own a heathen slave, were more squeamish about possessing a Christian. For this reason, although they allowed missionaries to teach their slaves the principles of Christianity, they would not allow them to be baptized. Later, men came

As elsewhere, North Carolina's slaves had the fewest rights and were assigned the hardest jobs. Performing all the countless tasks involved in running a plantation, they also mastered many highly skilled trades, and often their owners profited from renting out slaves' craftsmanship to other whites.

to see no inconsistency in a Christian slave, and the blacks were not only baptized but provided with a special balcony in local white churches.

As elsewhere, North Carolina slaves were assigned all the lowest, hardest, least-skilled labor. They cleared land and plowed fields, tended livestock, hauled firewood, performed the countless chores connected with tobacco farming—planting, hoeing, suckering, de-insecting, cutting, hanging, keeping fires (if needed) burning in the curing sheds, stripping, sorting, packing in hogsheads, transporting. If the master had vessels of his own, or those of his consignee called at his private wharf, slaves loaded the cargo.

In time slaves came to perform all the other skilled occupations that a remote plantation depended on—cooking, shoemaking, candle dipping, spinning, making brick, weaving, smithing, keeping house, charcoal burning, preparing herbs and simples in the stillroom, driving vehicles, tanning leather, fishing, waiting at table, manufacturing furniture, sewing. In the towns—still very few in number, of course—a slave might be apprenticed by his master to a skilled craftsman and thus learn a fine trade: wood carving, barbering, locksmithing, cabinetmaking, millwrighting. His skill could then be rented out for his master's profit.

A freedman with a skill was in a fortunate position to set up business for himself. With his profits, he might be able to buy his wife and children free, as well, and in time he might even acquire a slave or two of his own. But the unskilled freedman was nearly always reduced to the lowest of chores—carpet beating, odd jobbing, cutting firewood, emptying cesspools. And North and South, American chimneys were swept by free blacks.

On the continent of Europe, where flues were broader, grown men were employed in sweeping chimneys—sometimes licensed officials of the government. But English and American flues were too narrow for an adult to crawl through, and in large houses they were too complex to be cleaned with a long-handled device. The answer was "climbing boys," apprenticed to a master sweep at the age of five or six.

Before dawn, the master (usually black himself) would lead out his troop of little black children and wander the streets of town calling out his trade: "Sweep, sweep, ho-o-o-o!" Summoned to a house to perform his trade, he would tack up a blanket over the outside of his client's fireplace, then send one of his apprentices behind the blanket and up the flue. The child would squirm and struggle his way to the roof of the house, which might be two or three stories high, and out at the mouth of the chimney stack. As his small head popped out at the top, it was traditional for him to sing a little song of triumph—grateful that he had not scraped his flesh on a rough piece of brick or burned it on a too-hot passage or gotten stuck in a narrow elbow. Then he would start down, scraping at the encrusted flue walls with a triangular-bladed tool as he descended to the fireplace.

A sympathetic eyewitness of the work of one "pyjama-clad midget" described this descent:

> As the scrape, scrape was heard, the showers of soot fell behind the blanket, until at last the ebony figure appeared with a cone-shaped cap drawn down over his eyes and held out a grimy hand for the big round penny which awaited him below as his personal perquisite.

A kindly master might let the child keep his penny, but it was more usual for him to seize it as part of his own (very low) fee. The soot was also his, to be swept up, bagged, and later sold as fertilizer.

Often by the age of ten these climbing boys were too large for the narrow flues and were simply turned loose by an irresponsible master. If they stayed with their grim trade, they could expect to be despised and ostracized, even by other blacks. And in time they would probably meet an early death from tuberculosis or cancer—if they hadn't at some point gotten wedged into a too-tight passage and suffocated.

The Wealthy Planters

Some settlers, especially along the coastal area, had established decidedly comfortable estates for themselves. Although not many numerically, these "better sorts" came to have political influence out of proportion to their numbers, being appointed to seats on the council and sometimes to the governorship. Their private lives soon developed graciousness:

> The Planters by the richness of the Soil, live after the most easie and pleasant Manner of any People I have ever met with; for you shall seldom hear them Repine at any Misfortunes in life, except the loss of Friends, there being plenty of all Necessaries convenient for Life.

The homes of these wealthy planters reflected their prosperity. They copied the Georgian style of architecture and adapted it to smaller buildings, some of which were built of brick mortared with lime made from oyster shells. These houses were designed for warm weather, with wide halls and high ceilings. Most were two stories high, four large rooms on each floor—the parlor, dining room, and sitting rooms on the first floor and the bedrooms on the upper. Kitchens were either under the dining room in an aboveground basement or in a separate building joined with a covered runway. This latter system, popular throughout the South, enabled the family to escape the heat of cooking and was also a precaution against fire.

Most of these large houses were built on a bluff above a river or creek, approached from the land side by a drive lined with a graceful avenue of giant oak trees. To one side of the mansion were the barns, stables, and poultry houses, and still farther away were the slave quarters. If the water was deep enough to carry a vessel, there was probably a private wharf and boat shed at river's edge.

The planters' homes were beautifully furnished with belongings brought from England—tapestries, draperies, featherbeds, and silver plate and table service. Fireplaces in every room gleamed with brass or copper andirons, fenders, tongs, and shovels, while crystal decanters and cut-glass wine goblets cast a soft glow from mahogany sideboards.

Having much leisure, the rich planters—and even the not-so-rich loungers from the backcountry—adored sports and gaming. Wrote Dr. Brickell:

> The chiefest Diversions here are Fishing, Fowling; and Hunting Wild Beasts, such as Deer, Bears, Raccoons, Hares, Wild Turkies, with several other sorts. . . . *Horse-Racing* they are fond of, for which they

have Race-Paths near each Town, and in many parts of the Country. . . . They are much addicted to *Gaming*, especially at Cards and Dice, Hazard [dice game] and All-fours [card game], being the common Games they use . . . *Cock-Fighting* they greatly admire, which Birds they endeavor to procure from England and Ireland. . . . Wrestling, Leaping, and such Activities are much used by them; yet I never observed any Foot Races. *Dancing* they are all fond of, especially when they can get a Fiddle or Bag-pipe; at this they will continue Hours together. . . .

A diverse colony, filled with people of many different social classes, conditions of servitude, economic status, religion, and ethnic background, was slowly starting to unify itself and grow up.

CHAPTER FIFTEEN

Westward Expansion

England seemed to be always at war with either France or Spain. In 1739 it was Spain, a conflict brought about by the alleged grievances of an English sea captain named Robert Jenkins, whose ship had been boarded by Spanish officers in the West Indies. The officers had rifled the ship's hold, apparently looking for contraband, and when Jenkins protested this rough treatment, one of the Spaniards sliced off his ear. Ear in hand, Jenkins appealed to Parliament to redress his grievances, and the indignant legislators—spoiling for a fight after a long peace—declared war on Spain.

King George's War

The War of Jenkins' Ear, known in America as King George's War, started off with a bang. Called on to supply troops for this brawl, the North Carolina assembly voted to form four companies of one hundred men each, and appropriated £1,200 to outfit them. These troops were placed under the command of local officers—one of them James Innes, one of the three men who prompted the first Scots Highlanders to emigrate to North Carolina—and sailed for Jamaica to rendezvous with the Royal Navy and some British foot soldiers.

In command of the naval forces on this expedition was Rear Admiral Edward Vernon. The year before, Vernon, as a member of Parliament, had loudly condemned the timidity of the ministry in prosecuting the war and bragged that he could take Portobelo (near modern Colón, Panama) with six ships. When the ministry took him up on this boast, Vernon did better than his promise. With the men from six men-of-war, he attacked the wealthy Spanish city in November, 1739, and took it in a single day with the loss of only seven men.

With this stunning success behind him, the admiral had no trouble obtaining a fleet of 109 ships and land troops to the number of 12,000 men—mostly Americans. In January, 1741, the admiral sailed from Jamaica for Cartagena (a city on the Caribbean coast of modern Colombia).

But Admiral Vernon's luck had run out. His attack was quickly repulsed, and fever struck his troops. Thousands died. Out of four hundred North Carolinians who set out on this expedition, only Captain Innes and twenty-five men from the Cape Fear company are known to have returned to their native colony.

But one outcome of this ill-fated expedition was lasting. A young Virginia captain so admired his commander-in-chief that he decided to apply the admiral's name to a new estate he was building along the Potomac. Lawrence Washington was not well then, and when he died shortly after, he left Mount Vernon to his younger half-brother, George.

While these troops were serving the Caribbean, the Spanish moved into the Carolina sounds. Establishing a tent town on Ocracoke Island, they sent out a flotilla of small privateers to raid Carolina shipping. They were so bold and operated with such impunity that ship owners might see their vessels boarded and rifled while still within view of the shore.

In this crisis, the Royal Navy was elsewhere, but an English privateer, the *Duke William*, George Walker master, happened to be anchored in the Cape Fear when a Carolina sloop arrived with a tale of a hairbreadth escape from the Dons. Walker offered his ship's services to the Carolinians, and they agreed to put him and his crew on wages as long as they cruised their coast.

Setting out from the Cape Fear, Walker cruised for four months, from St. Augustine to the capes of Virginia. This show of strength seems to have alarmed the Spaniards, for they up and left in haste. Landing on Ocracoke, Walker destroyed a fortification the Dons had left there, and finding the sounds clear of enemy ships, he pronounced the region safe once more. Offered a 6,500-acre tract as a reward, Walker turned it down and sailed for home.

Six years later the Spaniards were back. Their favorite hunting ground this time was between the Cape Fear and Charleston, South Carolina. In June, 1747, they attacked and plundered Brunswick, left, and returned two months later for a three-day stay. Shipping was at a standstill before these depredations, and although a few naval vessels were sent to patrol the area, they did little good.

> Several small Sloops and Barcalonjos [reported Governor Johnston], came creeping along the shore from St. Augustine full of armed men, most Mulattoes and Negroes, their small Draught of water secured them from the attacks of the only ship of war on this station. . . . They killed several of His Majesty's subjects, burned some ships and several small Vessels, carried off some Negroes, and slaughtered a Vast number of Black Cattle and Hogs.

On September 4, 1748, a Spanish force suddenly popped up in the Cape Fear River and opened fire on the defenseless town of Brunswick. Many of the inhabitants fled from this third invasion. But apparently feeling that enough was enough, they then decided that this time they would fight back. They sent for the local militiamen to come to their aid. While the latter were mustering, the Spaniards plundered and destroyed freely, apparently in such confidence that they posted no guard. When eighty Carolinians crept back into their town two days later, they took the Dons by surprise. They were doing well against the invading privateersmen when one of the Spanish vessels, at anchor in the river, began firing on them. Then, for no known reason, the vessel blew up. Most of its officers and crew were killed, and the Carolinians easily seized the rest of the landing party. The Dons had another ship with them, however, and some of them escaped downriver in it.

After they had left, the Carolinians sold their captives into slavery and auctioned off the goods they had taken, using the money to help finance the construction of St. Philip's Church in Brunswick and St. James's Church in Wilmington. St. James's still displays a painting taken from one of the Spaniards, a head of Christ entitled "Ecce Homo," "Behold the Man."

The Scotch-Irish Arrive . . .

The Treaty of Aix-la-Chapelle put an end to King George's War, and the Carolinians were free to turn to things that interested them more—settlement and expansion.

The first group to arrive in this period, 1735, were the Scotch-Irish. Some, landing at Philadelphia, traveled west as far as the Shenandoah Valley, then headed south through the backcountry into the Piedmont of North Carolina. This route followed what was called the Great Wagon Road—not a highway in any sense but a reasonably followable trail that debouched north of what is now Winston-Salem. It had been used originally by the Indians—chiefly the Cherokee when raiding their northern cousins, the Iroquois—and was called the Great War Road. But wagons could negotiate it after a bumpy fashion, so it became as famous in its day as the Oregon Trail would become a century later.

Sometimes this journey took the Scotch-Irish two or three generations to accomplish. The first immigrant from Ulster might settle in one spot, perhaps Pennsylvania or Maryland. As his children grew up and married, they would move on farther south, perhaps to Virginia, only to have the next generation journey farther south again. Eventually, the height of the mountains blocked this movement, and expansion moved in the only direction left—west.

Other Scotch-Irish arrived in the Piedmont by way of Charleston or

North Carolina was prey to Spanish privateers in the War of Jenkins' Ear. Raiding up the Cape Fear River, they twice sacked Brunswick, only to be captured on their third assault. Proceeds from the capture built St. James Church shown here in Wilmington.

Wilmington. Geography was still shaping North Carolina's history, for the most navigable of her upland rivers did not flow directly into Albemarle, Bath, or other coastal-plain regions, but emptied far to the south. Since all colonial communications and commercial ties with the hinterland followed the easy river-valley routes, this meant that the newcomers were of more interest to South Carolina than to North. In time, this disconnection between coastal settlements and those of the backcountry would cost the colony an important rift in outlook—a lack of interdependence, a lack of sympathy.

Symbolic of this lack of interconnection was the new cattle industry that sprang up in the North Carolina backcountry. In early days, a farmer might own a few cattle along with horses and hogs, all of which he would mark with his own symbol—a brand for horses and cattle, an ear notch for hogs —and turn loose to forage for themselves. But now that the Piedmont had been opened for settlement, an area of clayey soil where tobacco did not thrive, men began to turn to cattle for their cash crop. Herds were enlarged—perhaps even improved a bit by selective breeding—and turned loose. Every year there would be a roundup, at a central collection point called a cowpen, after which the herd was driven to market—not in Albemarle but in South Carolina, Virginia, or even faraway Pennsylvania. In time this "ranching" system would become the mainstay of the great Southwest, but for the moment it symbolized chiefly that North Carolina was becoming two states of mind.

The Scotch-Irish, a prickly, aggressive people full of rude energy, formed the bulk of the settlers on the frontier—the wilderness scouts, the Indian traders and fighters, the "long hunters" probing the unexplored lands of the interior. Armed with the long rifle, invented by some unknown genius in Pennsylvania in the 1720's, they made excellent hunters and dangerous soldiers. Such Revolutionary War heroes as William R. Davie, Benjamin Cleveland, and Isaac Shelby were North Carolina Scotch-Irish. So were three American Presidents: James K. Polk, Andrew Johnson, and Old Hickory himself, Andrew Jackson.

Scotch-Irish settlers— Presbyterians from the north of Ireland—formed the bulk of the hardy frontiersmen. Clad in deerhide leggings and linsey-woolsey hunting shirt, armed with the accurate long rifle, these men hunted and explored the backcountry and led the march through the mountains to the West.

... Accompanied by the Germans

Around 1747, the second wave of German immigrants (counting von Graffenried's settlement as the first) arrived in the Piedmont, to be joined by some seasoned Pennsylvania Dutch. Between them and the many later waves of German immigrants, they settled a large arc of territory from the Charlotte region through that of Greensboro to Durham.

Less restless than their Scotch-Irish neighbors, who were still flooding in during the period of German immigration, the Germans tended to put down roots where they first landed and to devote themselves to farming. Wrote Governor Dobbs in 1755 of some Germans who had settled on his land:

> They raise horses, cows, and hogs with a few sheep, they raise Indian Corn, wheat, barley, rye, and oats, make good butter and tolerable cheese, and they have gone into indigo with good success, which they sell at Charles Town, having a waggon road to it tho' 200 miles distant. . . . They sow flax for their own use and cotton, and what Hemp they have sown is tall and good.

Not all the Germans were farmers, however. Some settled in villages, where they plied such homely trades as shoemaker, carpenter, baker, and tailor, and in time these villages would grow up to be the towns and manufacturing centers of the modern Piedmont.

Most interesting of the German settlers were the Moravians. These people take their name from Moravia, the region in central Europe that was originally part of the Holy Roman Empire and is now a district in Czechoslovakia. They belonged to a sect, *Unitas Fratrum* ("Unity of Brothers," or United Brethren), that could easily claim to be the oldest Protestant Church in the world, for it was founded by the Bohemian reformer John Huss shortly after 1400.

Like the Quakers, Moravians rejected oaths, war, and an established church, and they accepted the Bible as their only doctrinal authority. They stressed an austere life style as well, and preferred to live communally, dividing up the population of their communities into groups according to age and sex. Married couples had their own cottages, but the unmarried adults were separated from their families and lived in dormitory buildings called the Brothers' House and the Sisters' House. Both sexes dressed in subdued colors, and the women piously covered their heads with white caps. The community's income was divided up among the members according to need.

For two hundred years they thrived, but in the Thirty Years' War they were all but wiped out and forced underground for the next century. Finally, in the 1720's, they came under the protection of the Pietist Count Nikolaus Ludwig von Zinzendorf. He was interested in American colonization, and he sent a group of Moravians to the brand-new colony of Georgia (founded 1733). Finding themselves expected to bear arms against the Spanish in King George's War, Moravians abandoned this first settlement and moved to Pennsylvania in 1740, where they established the towns of Bethlehem, Nazareth, and Lititz.

Methodical, industrious, and quiet-loving (by contrast to the Quakers, whose principles were a thorn in the side to many colonies), the Moravians made ideal colonists. Lord Granville, the sole remaining proprietor, invited some of these Pennsylvanians to settle on his land, and their leader, Bishop August Gottlieb Spangenberg, picked out a tract in the area that is now Forsyth County. They called it Wachau after von Zinzendorf's estate in Saxony, but in time that was changed to Wachovia. In November, 1753, the first fifteen Moravians, hand-picked for their skills, arrived from Pennsylvania and set to work preparing Wachovia for the rest, who came later.

In the spring the community planted buckwheat, potatoes, flax, cotton, five kinds of grain, vegetables, and fruit trees, and acquired some livestock. They established a store to sell what they produced, and those of them who had special skills opened for business. In no time at all they were turning out pottery, clay pipes, wooden items, and other goods, which they either sold locally or shipped in wagons to Wilmington or Charleston.

Five years after this first settlement, called Bethabara, had been made, it was followed by another some miles away, Bethania. In 1766, a third Moravian settlement was made, named Salem. The first two never grew very large, but Salem thrived and was soon the largest center of religion, industry, and agriculture in the entire region.*

No other group got along with other settlers as well as the Moravians. In spite of their exotic life style and piety, they were recognized by act of Parliament as part of the established church. When necessary, they preached their sermons in English, although normally services were conducted in German, and administered sacraments freely to whoever requested them. Visitors came to the Moravians for medical or dental care (their settlement at Bethlehem, Pennsylvania, was the Continental Army's best hospital), took refuge among them from the Indians, bought their goods, and departed in peace and good cheer. They brought music to the Piedmont as well, in the form of sophisticated instruments and trained performers. They maintained their special kind of communal life and used German in their religious services until 1856.

* In 1849, Forsyth County was formed in this region, but the local people did not want the German community to serve as the county seat, so they made a fourth settlement a mile north of Salem and named it Winston. In 1913, the two settlements having grown together, the inhabitants voted to unite them as Winston-Salem. Bethabara and Bethania are villages today, a few miles northwest of the city.

The Indians of Western North Carolina

What had happened to the Siouan peoples who originally inhabited these clay hills? They suffered the usual difficulties of Indians in contact with white settlers—disease, cheating traders, loss of their hunting grounds. In 1754, the Catawba spoke bluntly to the colonial government:

> You Rot Your grain in Tubs, out of which you take and make Strong Spirits You sell it to our young men and give it them, many times; they get very Drunk with it this is the Very Cause that they often-times Commit those Crimes that is offencive to You and us. . . . I heartily wish You would do something to prevent Your People from Dareing to Sell or give them any of that Strong Drink. . . .

Perhaps it was drink that had weakened the Siouans so greatly, for their chief problem in the eighteenth century was the enmity of other Indian peoples, particularly the Iroquois, the Algonkian tribes of the Ohio Valley, and the Cherokee. This enmity was largely of their own making, for they had long made a habit of invading the hunting grounds of other people to steal their game and visit war upon them. "All the nations round about," wrote a Virginia observer, "bearing in mind the havock these Indians used formerly to make among their ancestors in the insolence of their power, did at length avenge it home upon them and make them glad to apply to this Government for protection."

The Tutelo moved closer to white settlements, putting themselves under the shield of the North Carolina and Virginia governments, and the whites endeavored to make peace. At last, in 1722, at a conference in Albany, New York, a treaty was effected between the northern tribes and these Siouan. Relieved by the release of this pressure, the Piedmont Indians gave way before the oncoming whites and began to migrate to Pennsylvania and New York.

So far the Cherokees, safe in their mountain fastnesses, had been immune to attack or pressure from the whites. Their own villages relatively free from assaults, they raided the Siouan tribes or their enemy kin, the Iroquois, at will. But their time would soon come.

For in 1748 a seventeen-year-old named William Ingles had made a settle-ment on the New River, which meanders through a mountain valley in western Virginia and North Carolina. The New River was a tributary of the Kanawha, and the Kanawha flowed into the Ohio, so that Ingles was settled on the western slope of the Appalachian Mountains, facing western waters. The mountain wall had been pierced, and henceforth all American settlement would flow west.

CHAPTER SIXTEEN

War in the Forest

It was autumn, 1753. Governor Robert Dinwiddie of Virginia, having learned that the French in Canada had sent soldiers to build forts along a tributary of the Ohio, was incensed. The Ohio Valley was Virginia's! Why, only a few years ago the Crown had granted a group of speculators—American and English—500,000 acres of land there, which they hoped to resell to new English-speaking settlers. Governor Dinwiddie himself was a member of this Ohio Company. How dared the French invade!

To express his displeasure and that of the government in London, Dinwiddie chose a young messenger named George Washington. Washington knew the backcountry—he'd been surveying there for five years, since he was sixteen—and moreover he held the rank of major in the colonial forces. To guide the major, Dinwiddie sent a French interpreter, frontiersman Christopher Gist, and a small bodyguard of militia. They were to warn the French commander, Jacques Legardeur de St. Pierre, that if he did not immediately evacuate His Majesty's royal colony of Virginia, troops would be sent to drive him out.

One-eyed Legardeur's reply was short and to the point: "We are here, and by God, we expect to stay here."

Young Major Washington had a perilous journey home, but he made it to Williamsburg by the middle of January, 1754. Dinwiddie had already dispatched a group of Virginians to build a fort at the Forks of the Ohio (modern Pittsburgh's Golden Triangle). He did not yet know—he would soon find out—that this Virginia fort had scarcely been completed before the French arrived in force and overwhelmed it, replacing the small structure with a larger one of their own, which they named Fort Duquesne. Nevertheless, Dinwiddie wished to send a strong force of militiamen to support the advance group.

He sought help from his colonial neighbors. But other colonies saw no reason to spend their money and risk their lives to secure land for Virginia speculators. Only North Carolina showed interest. Her assembly voted money for four hundred men.

While that was taking place, Washington and his tiny Virginia forces were marching through the mountains in the direction of Fort Duquesne (they knew about the French conquest by then). Learning that a French unit was advancing toward him, Washington and some Indian allies crept up on the unwary French, took them by surprise, and in the skirmish that followed killed several of them. When word reached Fort Duquesne of this ambush, a larger French force was sent out to catch the Virginians and revenge the first assault.

In a makeshift fortification, which the Virginians with grim humor called Fort Necessity, the French cornered Washington. After an all-day attack, they forced him to surrender. This, the only surrender Washington would ever sign, took place on July 3, 1754.

These two little incidents eventually ignited the worldwide conflict known in America as the French and Indian War.

Braddock's Defeat

The first North Carolina troops to be voted were put under the command of James Innes (who had led the Cape Fear Company against Cartagena in 1741), now a colonel. Innes and his men were sent to build a fort at the junction of Wills Creek and the Potomac River, which was named Fort Cumberland after William Augustus, Duke of Cumberland, the royal prince who was commander-in-chief of the British army.* Henceforth Fort Cumberland (modern Cumberland, Maryland) would be the jumping-off place for expeditions against, and journeys to, the Forks.

On May 9, 1755, a short, burly, sixty-year-old Englishman arrived at Fort Cumberland at the head of two regiments of British regulars. Major General Edward Braddock had been sent by the government in London to see what the regulars could do about throwing the French out of the Ohio Valley.

The colonies had been called on to contribute troops, supplies, and money. North Carolina was completely unprepared for war. Governor Arthur Dobbs replied to the request of the London government that the militia of his colony was unorganized and untrained. Not half of the men had guns, and those they had were in bad condition, being used only to hunt game. There was not a pound of public gunpowder or shot in the province. He asked the king for help, because the province had no credit and must pay double for arms and ammunition bought from merchants.

The king sent one thousand guns, and the assembly voted eight thousand pounds and one hundred men, exclusive of officers, to join General Brad-

* This was an ironic choice of name for a Highlander like Innes, for Cumberland was the officer who had ordered the brutal suppression of the Highlands in 1746. He was labeled Cumberland the Butcher by the Scots.

General Braddock's disciplined regulars were no match for the Indians and Frenchmen behind forest cover. Mowed down by an invisible enemy, they soon broke and fled. Their commander, carried off the field mortally wounded, died and was secretly buried.

dock in his expedition against Fort Duquesne. The governor's son, Major Edward Brice Dobbs, was placed in command of these troops.

General Braddock had had no experience in wilderness fighting. He considered the colonial troops completely inadequate and dismissed the Indians as useless. He allowed George Washington to serve under him as a volunteer civilian aide, but he did not believe that the young Virginian had much expert advice to give. The expedition had to build a twelve-foot-wide road through the wilderness so they could haul their supply wagons and siege artillery, but halfway to the fort, Braddock left part of his equipment behind under his second-in-command and pushed on.

Finally, on July 9, the British troops drew near Fort Duquesne, marching down the road they had cut, massed together in neat, solid rows. Eight miles from the fort, they had to ford the Monongahela River. As the troops marched up from the water on the opposite side, the French and their Indian allies opened fire from ambush.

The English regulars, trained to blind obedience, stood fast and even fired a volley or two. But as the battle raged on, and they saw their comrades mowed down by an invisible enemy, they broke. Running every which way, they were an easy target for the hidden French, easy victims for the Indians to run down in the forest and dispatch with the tomahawk. The colonial troops took severe losses too, and Washington himself had two horses shot from under him, four bullets through his clothes. Miraculously he escaped without a wound, but his commanding officer was not so lucky. Mortally wounded, Braddock was carried off by his hastily retreating army, and three days later he died. Washington ordered the army's wagons driven over the grave so that the Indians would not find it and dig up the corpse.

All this time, Major Dobbs and the North Carolina regiment had been off on a scouting expedition and missed the battle entirely. After receiving word, they retreated to Fort Cumberland and joined Colonel Innes.

Indian Troubles

After Braddock's defeat, the whole of the frontier was overrun with triumphant Indians, killing, burning, driving the whites back east. Along the Catawba and Yadkin rivers in the Piedmont they spread out, bringing destruction and death to every settler they encountered.

At the behest of Governor Dobbs, the assembly hastily voted to authorize the creation of a force to protect the outlying areas and to construct a fort near a tributary of the Yadkin (near modern Statesville). Men and fort were put under the command of Major Hugh Waddell. Completed in 1756, the work was named Fort Dobbs in honor of the governor.

This show of force helped some, but it was not enough to prevent whole regions of the Piedmont from becoming depopulated. Then, in the spring of 1758, a new British expedition against Fort Duquesne was mounted, this one nearly three times the size of Braddock's force.

In command was a tough, plodding, methodical Scot named John Forbes. Along with a strong unit of regulars, Forbes commanded five thousand Americans, three hundred of them North Carolinians. Leading this contingent was Major Waddell.

Like Braddock, Forbes was forced to build a road as he went to haul his cannon and supplies. But this time he chose to march through Pennsylvania, and instead of trying to make march, road building, and assault in one leap, he took his time, pausing to build forts and caches for his supplies as he went along. Thus it was November before he got to within forty miles of the French fort.

Now Forbes had to make a decision. Should they go into winter quarters or continue on to Duquesne? It would help to know what condition the French were in. The general offered an award of £500 to anyone who would capture an enemy who could give them the necessary information.

Waddell and his men, regularly employed on reconnoitering parties, fell in with just such an Indian and took him back to the British camp. Yes, the native told them, the French position had been badly weakened by desertion and lack of supplies. Forbes decided to push on.

On November 25, an advance party of Americans under the command of George Washington arrived at the forks to find the French fort a smoking ruin. The garrison had blown it up and fled down the Ohio.

Meanwhile, the Cherokee had gone on the warpath against the Carolinas. Originally pro-English because their enemies the Shawnee were pro-French, they had sent a band of warriors to assist Forbes, only to desert in disgust at the plodding pace of his advance. They had also suffered severely from the depredations of the backcountry whites, especially of Virginia and South Carolina, and when the French began to prod them to change sides, they did so. Turning about, they launched war parties on the beleaguered Piedmont. Soon it was 1755–56 all over again, with scalping bands roaming about at will. Men took refuge with the Moravians at Bethabara and Bethania, where church bells and watchmen's horns tended to make the Cherokee wary.

Even more vigorous was the Cherokee campaign against South Carolina, where they besieged and took a colonial fort in the mountains. In revenge for ambassadors wantonly murdered by whites, they killed an equal number of the South Carolinian garrison of this force and tortured to death a number of prisoners. Two expeditions of regulars marched into the mountains in pursuit of the Cherokee, succeeding only in burning a few cornfields and upside-down-basket houses before marching away again. At last in December, 1761, the Cherokee, their thirst for satisfaction momentarily slaked, agreed to a peace treaty.

The white man's war was over in America by then, too, and peace seemed to rule in the mountains and forests. But the Cherokee, their strongholds no longer immune to assault, had been alerted to the white menace. From this time on, they would play down their enmity to other Indian peoples. Now they knew it was the whites they had to combat.

CHAPTER SEVENTEEN

The Stamp Act

By 1764, Governor Arthur Dobbs was seventy-five years old. To help him with his duties, the king sent Colonel William Tryon to North Carolina with a commission as lieutenant governor. When the old governor died a year later, Tryon became governor of North Carolina in his own right.

An able and energetic man, Tryon was inclined to tackle all problems head-on, like the professional soldier that he was. He might have done some excellent things for North Carolina if he had not come to his appointment at the very moment when all colonial governors were being caught in a squeeze between their official duties and colonial demands for self-determination.

Passage

When Tryon took office in April, 1765, the chief topic of conversation among North Carolinians was the Stamp Act that Parliament had threatened to pass (*had* passed, actually, but the news had not yet crossed the Atlantic). This act, requiring that all official documents be made out on paper that carried a government stamp, would put a direct impost on every aspect of colonial life. A man could not marry, draft a will, ship a cargo of goods, go to court, read a newspaper, receive a college diploma, or do almost anything else without paying a tax on it. Moreover, if he violated this act, he would be brought before a court of admiralty and tried by royal judges, who sat without a jury. During the year's warning that Parliament had given the colonists, there had been much debating about the idea of taxation. Many Americans took it for granted that Parliament had the right to impose a tax on them. Others hotly denied it. On the previous October 31 (1764), the North Carolina assembly had passed a resolution stating, "We esteem it our inherent right and exclusive privilege to impose our own taxes."

When the new governor asked the speaker of the assembly, John Ashe, what the people would do about the Stamp Act, Ashe answered emphatically, "Resist unto blood and death."

The governor dismissed the assembly until November, hoping things would cool off. Instead, they heated up. As news of the actual passage reached America, colony after colony exploded. Massachusetts issued a call to a Stamp Act Congress, to meet in New York. In Virginia, Burgess Patrick Henry, making his famed if-this-be-treason speech, proposed a set of resolutions flatly denying Parliament's right to tax the colonies, and the house passed it. Rhode Island, learning of Virginia's action, stoutly backed her up and added a refinement: Officers of the colony were not to enforce the act. In North Carolina, men formed themselves into patriotic groups called the Sons of Liberty.

Resistance

The summer of 1765 was the hottest in the memory of North Carolina residents. Crops failed, and ships were not allowed to carry out any bread except what was absolutely necessary for the crews. To make matters worse, an epidemic of yellow fever broke out in New Bern, and Governor Tryon himself was sick with malarial fever. In spite of their troubles, however, the Stamp Act remained first in the minds of the people.

Suspension of their assembly prevented North Carolina from sending delegates to the Stamp Act Congress, but public demonstrations against the act were held in Edenton, New Bern, Cross Creek (center of the Highland settlement), and other towns. On October 19 about five hundred men assembled at Wilmington and burned in effigy a former prime minister

The Stamp Act required that all official papers—diplomas, ships' manifests, newspapers—had to carry these stamps. When the speaker of the North Carolina assembly was asked what people would do about this act, he retorted grimly, "Resist unto blood and death."

Hanging in effigy was a favorite form of protesting the Stamp Act. On October 19, 1765, Wilmington patriots strung up an effigy of a former prime minister. A month later a crowd of four hundred forced their stamp master to resign his post.

whom they mistakenly blamed for the Stamp Act (actually he had voted against it). About two weeks later they met again. This time they had made an effigy which they called Liberty and placed it in a coffin. Solemnly, with muffled mourning drums beating, they marched to the graveyard with the coffin on their shoulders while the town bell rang a doleful knell.

Before they buried the "corpse," however, one man knelt beside the coffin to feel the "pulse" of the effigy, and

> when finding some Remains of Life, they returned back to a Bonfire ready prepared, placed the effigy before it in a large, Two-arm'd Chair, and concluded the Evening with great Rejoicings, on finding that Liberty had still an Existence. . . .

In November, Dr. William Houston, who had been appointed stamp master for North Carolina, went to Wilmington. Three or four hundred people met him with drums beating and colors flying and escorted him into the courthouse. They forced him to sign a paper resigning his office, and that evening they celebrated with bonfires and toasts. In Cumberland, New Bern, and Duplin the people showed their feelings in the same fashion, burning effigies of Dr. Houston and celebrating Liberty.

Governor Tryon, although still ill, was well informed as to what was taking place. He sent letters to about fifty of the most prominent Sons of Liberty inviting them to dinner on November 18. After a lavish banquet, he expressed his hope that no violence would be done when the stamps arrived. If they would only be sensible and quiet, he urged, he would win from the London government "favorable indulgence and exception" for North Carolina—so that, while other colonies' shipping was held up for lack of clearance papers (which had to be printed on stamped paper), North Carolina would be free to profit from commerce. He promised to do anything he could to keep the tax from being a hardship on anyone, even promising to recompense any damage out of his own pocket.

It was a bribe, of course, but a shrewd move. No other colonial governor came so close to splitting the Stamp Act opposition. But in the end it failed, too. The guests said they would consider his proposal and reply to it the next day. When a committee arrived at the governor's home the following morning, they presented him with their reply: They appreciated Tryon's position and his desire to govern the colony so well, yet they could never submit to part of the act (accepting the stamps) without submitting to the whole, and "We can never consent to be deprived of the invaluable Privilege of a Trial by Jury."

In spite of this rebuff, Governor Tryon continued to use all his political ploys to try to placate the people of North Carolina. When a general muster of the militia was held in February, 1766, he prepared a feast for the men —a whole ox to be barbecued and barrels of beer to be opened. After the drill, he generously invited everyone to help themselves. The men rushed to the tables, turned over the barrels, and poured the beer on the ground. Then they threw the ox into the river without carving a single piece of it.

Attempt at Enforcement

Shenanigans broke the monotony but could not bring much relief. Life was hard in North Carolina during the life of the Stamp Act. Trade was at a standstill. Tobacco could not be shipped. Courts were closed. Newspapers and books could not be printed. Then in January, 1766, it all came to a head.

Early that month H.M.S. *Viper* seized three merchant vessels anchored at Brunswick for not having stamped clearance papers. With the ships' papers in his hand, William Dry, the local collector of customs, appealed to the colony's attorney general for a decision as to the disposal of the case. In mid-February, the latter replied that the ships should be sent to the Vice-Admiralty Court in Halifax, Nova Scotia.

That was too much for the Cape Fear counties. On February 18, men met at Wilmington, chose Cornelius Harnett (a Son of Liberty) as their leader, and formed an "Association Against the Stamp Act." They then marched to Brunswick, posted a guard around Governor Tryon's house, and seized Collector William Dry. Ransacking the collector's desk, they found the confiscated ships' papers.

So far so good, but Harnett was not strong enough to do more. On February 20, however, when his followers had been reinforced to number one thousand, he acted. Sweeping down to the anchorage, the "Association" swarmed aboard the *Viper* and forced her captain to release the impounded vessels. With both captain and collector in their power, they extracted a promise that henceforth Brunswick would be stamp-free.

The following day, while the main body of the "Association" rounded up all smaller fry of customs officers, Harnett and sixty followers went after William Pennington, the comptroller of customs, who had taken refuge in Tryon's house.

The soldier-governor stood firm. Pennington was under his protection, and he would not send him out. Harnett, looking Tryon in the eye, replied grimly that he and his men would seize Pennington by force if they had to. The governor still refused to yield, but at that juncture Pennington himself appeared and surrendered. Accompanied by the cheering "Association," he was marched to the center of town, where he swore a public oath that he would no longer execute the hated act.

Repeal

Meanwhile, in England, where trade was disrupted by the trade boycott that the colonies had instituted, merchants were besieging Parliament to repeal the act. Viewing in astonishment the continent-wide furore the measure had created, the legislators were inclined to agree that the Stamp Act was unenforceable. They voted for repeal, and on March 18, 1766, it was signed by George III.

On June 25, Governor William Tryon issued a proclamation announcing the news to North Carolina. The people felt that the colonies had won a victory and that the Stamp Act would be both the beginning and the end of any effort on the part of England to tax them. They divided up Mecklenburg County and made a new county, which they named Tryon in honor of the governor.

CHAPTER EIGHTEEN

The Rebellion of the Regulators

U p to this time there had been no permanent capital for the province of North Carolina. Bath was still used frequently, but often the governor lived at one place and the assembly met at another, while the treasurer might reside on a plantation in a quite different part of the colony. Several governors had tried to get the assembly to designate a town as the capital, but political squabbles always resulted in disagreement. When the question came up again in 1766, the delegates from Hillsboro in the Piedmont seemed strong enough to have it named as the capital. This so frightened the delegates from the eastern sections of Albemarle and Cape Fear that, instead of each area fighting for it, they compromised and voted together for New Bern.

Official Residence for the Governor

With this business settled to his satisfaction, Governor Tryon at once set about attaining his personal dream: a palace suitable for a royal governor. Pleased with the recent repeal of the Stamp Act, the assemblymen were in such a generous mood that in November, 1766, they voted £5,000 for this project. Since the treasury was practically bankrupt, the money was appropriated from the school and church funds and was to be repaid by putting a tax of twopence a gallon on all wine, rum, and liquor not imported from England. The governor was given the power to design and contract for construction of the building.

Governor Tryon turned all his attention to the pleasant task of supervising erection of this official residence. He commissioned John Hawks from Lincolnshire, England, to design it, and Hawks came to North Carolina to carry out his assignment. Called "the first professional architect to remain in America," he is thought to have designed a number of other buildings in North Carolina, including New Bern's John Wright Stanley House, now a museum, and the Coor-Gaston-Walker House. He is known to have supervised completion of the second Craven County courthouse. However, none of these buildings matched the magnificence of the governor's palace.

The palace was to include not only the governor's official residence but also the statehouse, assembly hall, council chamber, and public offices. For the main structure of a symmetrical compound, Hawks designed a two-story brick house, eighty-seven feet wide and fifty-nine feet deep. Above the door at roof level was a large white pediment displaying the royal coat of arms. Flanking this building on either side were two smaller two-story wings connected with the central house by semicircular colonnades. One wing contained the servants' quarters and a laundry. The other was to be used as a granary and hayloft.

The roof was shingled, which at that time was considered more beautiful than tile or slate. Two wells with pumps furnished the water. The grand staircase was lighted by a low glass dome, and over the vestibule door was the inscription in Latin: "A free and happy people, opposed to cruel tyrants, has given this edifice to virtue. May the house and its inmates, as an example for future ages, here cultivate the arts, order, justice, and the laws."

North Carolinians had a right to be proud of their statehouse. Tryon's Palace, as it is known today, has often been considered one of the most beautiful government houses in America.

Governor Tryon had soon spent the £5,000 the assembly had granted him. In order to persuade the members to give him more money, the governor and his lady, helped by Mrs. Tryon's beautiful sister, Esther Wake, gave brilliant balls and dinner parties for members of the assembly. At such events the governor craftily suggested that the assembly could raise the necessary funds for his palace by levying a poll tax of two shillings for three years. A poll tax, or "head money," is a flat sum collected from everyone without regard to his income or wealth. But the inequities of it did not bother the dazzled assemblymen. Before the building was finished in 1770, they had appropriated an additional £10,000 by this means.

Unrest in the Backcountry

Not everyone in North Carolina approved of this splendid new building. In the backcountry of the province, the Piedmont and the mountains, men considered it a waste of money—a waste of *their* money. Since the Piedmont had become more heavily populated than the tobacco-growing coastal plain, the poll tax would lay a heavier burden on this land of small farmers and craftsmen than it would on the wealthier planters.

Moreover, the Piedmont had few, if any, connections with New Bern. When westerners traded, they traveled down the river valleys to Charleston or Wilmington. "Not one man in twenty of the four most populous counties will ever see this famous house when built . . ." wrote one Piedmonter, "as their connections and trade . . . naturally center in South Carolina."

But the governor's "palace" and the poll tax were only symbols of a deeper discontent among the backcountry people. The political system in North Carolina was heavily pitched against them.

The basic unit of representation was the county. Hence, the number of counties erected in a region governed the number of representatives it had in the assembly. Since it was the assembly that created new counties, and the coastal-plain voters controlled the assembly, the Piedmonters could not win. As fast as new counties were carved out of old ones in the Piedmont, new ones were also added to those along the coast. In 1771, half the population of North Carolina lived in seven western counties with a total representation in the assembly of 17 votes. The other half, easterners all, had 61 votes.

Moreover, people in these regions did not even elect local officials, for all county officers were appointees. The governor appointed justices of the peace for the county courts, and they in turn appointed (or nominated for the governor to appoint, which amounted to the same thing) sheriffs, overseers of roads, constables, town commissioners, militia officers, and other officeholders. Many justices of the peace were also assemblymen, named to their posts for political favors, and others had bought their jobs outright, hoping to get rich from the fees they charged the poor. Almost without exception, these local officials were outsiders in the regions where they served, sometimes outsiders even in the province.

Many of these officers were ruthless in the execution of their duty. If a man did not have money to pay his taxes—voted by an assembly in which he was not fairly represented—the sheriff might seize his property and sell it for the amount of the tax due. Hardship was no excuse. A family's only cow or horse might be taken, leaving them helpless to farm.

In 1768, thirty citizens of Orange and Rowan counties presented a petition to the assembly, asking relief from the poll tax. They had been continually "Squeezed and oppressed," they said, and although a few shillings might seem "triffling" to "Gentlemen Rowling in affluence," to poor people it sometimes meant that a family was stripped of "Bed and Bedclothes yea their Wives Petticoats" in order to pay.

That same year ninety-nine people in another Piedmont county petitioned to be relieved of their clerk:

His extortions are burthensome of all that fall into his power as he takes double and treble his due. And tho' it is true he purchased his office . . . and gave to the amount of one hundred and fifty pounds, yet it's unreasonable we should bear the expense by way of extortion.

The Regulators

One of the most hated of these outsiders occupying local offices was Edmund Fanning, assemblyman of Orange County. A native of New York, he had been appointed by his friend Governor Tryon to a superior-court judgeship, a colonelcy in the militia, and an Orange County registership of deeds. He despised the common people, and they didn't think much of him. Rednap Howell, an Orange County schoolteacher, satirized him in a ballad that was still being sung in the 1820's:

> When Fanning first to Orange came,
>   He look'd both pale and wan:
> An old patch'd coat upon his back,
>   An old mare he rode on.
> Both man and mare wa'nt worth five pounds,
>   As I've been often told;
> But by his civil robberies,
>   He's lac'd his coat with gold.

In August, 1766, at a meeting of the county court at Hillsboro, a paper was circulated among the citizens present. It called on them to attend a general meeting in November, which would inquire into the oppressions and extortions of local officials.

Most assemblymen of the county admitted that the people did have grievances that needed looking into. One assemblyman, however, said he was not responsible to the people and refused to have his conduct judged by "the shallow understanding of the mob." This was Edmund Fanning.

Nothing much came of this first petition, but later—when it was labeled Regulator Advertisement Number One—it was regarded as the opening step in the campaign of the Regulators.

Formally organized in March, 1768, the Regulators were a group of local people who banded together to oppose illegal taxation and exorbitant fees. Their manifesto, drawn up early in 1768, did not deny the right of anyone to tax them or to charge them fees. It only stated that they would not pay more than the law allowed. They were determined to have public officers under better "regulation" than they had been.

Three backcountrymen took the lead in the formation of the Regulators: Herman Husband, Rednap Howell, and James Hunter. Husband, a Quaker, was a native of Maryland. He was shrewd, industrious, thrifty, and better educated than most of the people in the backcountry. Howell, a schoolteacher, was witty and good-natured, and had a talent for writing humorous poetry (he authored "When Fanning First to Orange Came," quoted previously). His sharply satiric verse kept the people in the backcountry laughing and singing jokes about the appointed officials. Hunter, a man of action, thought that petitions to the governor were too slow. He wanted to use force.

First Blood

The Regulators had hardly been organized before they were called into action. Late in March, 1768, the sheriff seized a Regulator's horse, saddle, and bridle for taxes and took them to Hillsboro. About sixty Regulators, led by Husband and Hunter, followed him and rescued the mare. They then marched to Fanning's house and fired their guns at the roof to let him know that they held him responsible.

Nothing much happened immediately. In May, the regulators drew up Regulator Advertisement Number Eleven, which regretted the violence of the previous incident, proclaimed the members' loyalty to the king and the law, and denounced only the "practices of nefarious and designing men." Hunter and Howell carried this petition to Brunswick and presented it to the governor.

Tryon, who had admitted in a private letter that more than half the taxes collected by the sheriffs had been unaccounted for, would not publicly acknowledge the justice of the petitioners' grievances. He dismissed the pair with the advice that they should give up the name "Regulators" and pay their taxes like good citizens. Privately, however, he admonished local officers against excessive charges and ordered publication of a list of legal fees, so men would know what was actually due.

In September, court met at Hillsboro. Husband and three of his followers had been arrested for inciting rebellion, but that news was almost offset by word that Fanning had also been haled into court. The charge: taking a six-shilling fee when the legal amount was two and eightpence. Excitement spread throughout Regulator country, and nearly four thousand persons poured into the little town. Taking alarm, Tryon decided to attend court himself, and arrived at the head of 1,400 militia.

The outcome was something of a vindication for the Regulators. Husband was acquitted, his followers convicted and sentenced to fines and short terms of imprisonment. Fanning was found guilty and fined one penny and costs, and he resigned his office. Tryon, hoping to calm the excitement, released the prisoners and pardoned their fines.

This modicum of success, instead of inducing the Regulators to return home satisfied, merely encouraged them to press on with their campaign for justice. Their numbers were swelling. In the 1769 elections, Orange, Anson, Granville, and Halifax counties returned only Regulator delegates, one of them Herman Husband for Orange. Incidents of violence and disorder were also on the increase, and at the next meeting of the court at Hillsboro, the docket was full of cases involving Regulators.

Again the Regulators poured into town, but this time there was no militia to make them cautious. Husband, Hunter, and Howell led a delegation of 150 men into the courtroom, where they commandeered all the best seats. One of their spokesmen then rose and announced to the judge that, since Regulators could not obtain justice in the province's courts, they would find it elsewhere.

Most of them left after the speech, but soon the ones who remained began to yell and go into action. They drove the judge from his bench, whipped an attorney, pulled another official through the streets. Edmund Fanning, unfortunately for him, happened to be in court. He tried to hide behind the judge's bench, but the infuriated Regulators dragged him out by his heels, hauled him about the town, whipped him, and ransacked his house. Then, with all the "better sort" in hiding, the Regulators raged through the streets, breaking windows, burning buildings, and terrorizing everyone they met.

The Battle of Alamance Creek

When the next assembly met, the chief topic of conversation was the Hillsboro Riot. Governor Tryon spoke heatedly about it and persuaded the assembly to pass a riot act that would outlaw persons who resisted arrest and give the governor power to use the militia against them. Tryon had Husband expelled from the assembly on charges of libel, but he was afraid to let him go back to Orange County, so he had him jailed at New Bern instead. Since the grand jury there was unable to find a true bill against him, Husband had to be released.

Meanwhile, news of the riot act had spread through Regulator country. Instead of putting the fear of God into the insurgents, as it was supposed to do, it roused them to greater anger than ever. The backcountry people swarmed to their support. They swore they would pay no more taxes, they would have no more judges and lawyers and courts. As for Fanning, they declared him an outlaw, to be shot down like a dog by the first man who recognized his face.

While the backcountry was still in this mood, the assembly met again in December, 1770, in the magnificent new governor's palace that had sparked the revolt in the first place. In an effort to weaken the Regulators, the legislators voted to divide Orange County and make three new counties. Parts of Orange, Cumberland, and Johnston counties were put together to form Wake County, named in honor of Governor Tryon's wife (née Margaret Wake). Another part of Orange and Rowan was called Guilford, and the

At the Battle of Alamance Creek, the ill-armed Regulators were driven into a nearby wood, which was then set on fire. Twelve men were made prisoner, six of them hanged, and the backcountry rebellion was crushed for good.

southern section was cut off and renamed Chatham, for the former British prime minister William Pitt, earl of Chatham.

Then it was time to take action against the insurgents.

The governor issued a proclamation in February, 1771, forbidding all merchants to supply anyone with powder, shot, or lead. The colony's own supplies of gunpowder, flints, blankets, and other military equipment he ordered sent to Colonel Hugh Waddell at Salisbury. In spring he called out the militia.

Meanwhile, the Regulators had learned of the colony's shipment of military stores and realized that these supplies were to be used against them. Since they were to be deprived of arms by the governor's embargo, they decided to serve the government's troops the same way. Nine young men who lived near Cabarrus blacked their faces, to avoid recognition, and set out to find the wagon train. On May 2, they discovered the supply wagons camped at Phifer's Hill. Descending on them, they captured the drivers, smashed the kegs of powder, and tore the blankets to pieces. Their leader, Major James White, fired his pistol into the remaining boxes of ammunition, sending them sky high.

When news of this action reached Governor Tryon, he offered a pardon to anyone who would identify the men. Two half brothers turned informant, and the other "Black Boys" fled to Georgia.

On May 13, Governor Tryon and his troops crossed the Haw River and camped on the banks of Great Alamance Creek (near modern Burlington). They were joined by more than two thousand militiamen from both eastern and western counties. About then, Husband, Howell, and Hunter must have realized that the jig was up, for they slipped quietly away.

On May 16, 1771, a large group of Regulators approached the governor's camp and sent him a last request that he listen to their grievances. Tryon replied that since they were in a state of rebellion against the king, he would talk with them only when they had laid down their arms. If they surrendered within an hour, he said, there would be no bloodshed—that was the most they could expect.

The hour passed. No word was received from the Regulators.

Tryon then sent his aide to say that unless they gave him their leaders as prisoners and dispersed, he would fire upon them. The Regulators retorted, "Fire and be damned!"

Tryon gave the order to fire, and when the militiamen did not obey at once, he rose in his stirrups and shouted: "Fire! Fire on them or on me!"

At the first volley, many of the Regulators fled. A good number of them were not armed, and few had expected to fight an actual battle. Nevertheless, at first, the remainder gave as many casualties as they took. Then, after about half an hour, they were forced back into a nearby wood, where they took refuge behind trees, Indian fashion. Governor Tryon's men surrounded the woods and set them on fire, to force the rebels out. Some came, surrendering reluctantly. Others preferred death. (A Moravian report of the battle says that some of the wounded were roasted alive.) Those who managed to escape fled from the area.

The militia pursued the fleeing Regulators for a mile beyond their camp, taking what horses, provisions, and ammunition they left behind. The next day the dead were buried (nine killed on each side), and prayers were said in thanksgiving for the victory.

A Regulator named James Few, taken prisoner in the battle, was brought before Governor Tryon. The man was well known for his curious beliefs—among them that he had been sent by Heaven to liberate his country and that he was to start in North Carolina. The governor told Few that if he would take the oath to uphold the law and pay his taxes, he would be pardoned. If not, he would be hanged.

The young man refused to take the oath. Tryon did not want to execute the half-mad rebel. When the rope was actually around the man's neck, the governor gave him one last chance to reconsider. Again Few refused. Governor Tryon turned away in exasperation, and James Few was "swung into eternity."

A detachment of the militia under Colonel Hugh Waddell marched through the countryside, forcing people to take an oath of allegiance to the colonial government. On June 9, Tryon returned to Hillsboro for the trials of twelve prisoners seized at Alamance Creek. A special court had been set up. All twelve were convicted and condemned to hang. Tryon pardoned six and turned his back on the others, who were quickly strung up. Then the governor let it be known that pardon would be extended to all not-as-yet-captured Regulators who would lay down their arms and submit to his authority. More than six thousand complied. One thousand others, feeling that reform of the North Carolina system was now impossible, fled through the mountains to the Tennessee country just opening up.

Like so many of his enemies, Edmund Fanning left North Carolina, too. That declaration of outlawry passed on him by people who could always lay their hands on a gun had never been rescinded.

Omitted from Tryon's pardon—indeed, the governor offered a reward for their capture—were the energetic ringleaders, Herman Husband, Rednap Howell, and James Hunter. The trio had escaped, however. Husband fled to his native Maryland and later journeyed to Pennsylvania. Howell returned to his home province of New Jersey. Hunter, after a few months in Maryland, returned to North Carolina.

Many of those Regulators who stayed on in North Carolina later fought bravely in the Revolutionary War, some on the Tory (Loyalist) side, some on the Whig (Patriot) side. The Regulator movement had nothing to do with independence from England.

The Two Governors

As for William Tryon, he had already gotten a new job as governor of the rich province of New York. His work in North Carolina completed—or so he felt—he sailed on June 30, 1771. When he arrived in New York he met Josiah Martin, who was to take his place in North Carolina. The two governors had a long talk.

Martin, like Tryon, had been a lieutenant colonel in the British army (as were many other colonial governors—Great Britain, which had few generalships to distribute, had to find *some* way to reward colonels for their loyal military service). Thirty-four years old, well educated, he had strong family connections in England. The two military gentlemen evidently agreed on the course of action to be pursued in North Carolina, for when Martin arrived in New Bern in August, he was quite confident that he knew how to handle the job.

He could not possibly have guessed that he was to be North Carolina's last colonial governor.

CHAPTER NINETEEN

Times of Trouble

It was the summer of 1774—the emigrant ship *Baliol* lay at anchor in the port of Campbelltown, Kintyre, western Scotland. On board were a fifty-two-year-old woman and her equally middle-aged husband, on their way to North Carolina. It had taken them three years to sell their property and pack up their movables for the journey: their silver, their furniture, their books. For this couple were no gillies in belted plaid and deerskin brogues, with only a leather purse to their name, but gentry—he the son of a minor chief, she a woman who was already famous in Scottish history.

Legendary Heroine

Flora MacDonald—although married now, she was still "MacDonald," for her husband Allan belonged to the same clan—had helped save the life of the Highlands' romanticized darling, Prince Charles Edward Stuart, the Young Pretender, best known as Bonnie Prince Charlie.

That had happened nearly thirty years earlier, in June, 1746, on the island of South Uist (pronounced yew-ist) in the Outer Hebrides. Flora, then a young woman of twenty-four, was approached by one Captain Felix O'Neill. A close comrade of the prince, he had helped his master escape capture by fleeing to the Hebrides. Now the captain desperately needed help in getting him back to the mainland again.

The MacDonalds, loyal to the Stuart family, had been "out" in the Rising of 1745 in great numbers. This little eight-month rebellion, which started in a lonely glen at the head of Loch Eil in Inverness Shire in the summer of 1745, brought clansmen flocking to the prince's standard and at first had astounding success against the unprepared British government. The Highlanders defeated several scratch forces sent against them and marched into England as far as Derby, intent on putting Charles's father on the English throne. But then, unnerved by their success, the Highlanders faltered and began to demand a return to their own land, and the rebel army retreated to Scotland. The following April, at Culloden Moor, outside Inverness, the Duke of Cumberland and a strong detachment of regulars cornered the wild Highlanders and butchered them mercilessly. Charles fled the battlefield, and like everyone else who got away alive, he went into hiding.

The British were frantic to get their hands on him. They offered a reward of £30,000—a fabulous sum for the day, enough to make a man wealthy for life—for information leading to Charles's capture.* Instead, the Highlanders spirited him from hand to hand. Says the old Jacobite song:

> We watched you in the gloamin' hour,
> We watched you in the mornin' gray.
> Though thirty thousand pounds they'd gie,
> There was nane that wad betray.

Flora, asked for help, was eager to provide it. But how?

Cumberland had ships of war cruising the coast, watching the shores of sea lochs and islands like so many cats at mouseholes. But something had to be done soon, for the duke also had troops making a sweep of South Uist, searching every foot of ground, every house. Soon they would come to the cave where Charles was hiding.

Flora and the captain worked up a plan. She would obtain a pass to go to the mainland with her Irish maid, "Betty Burke"—the prince in disguise. Flora was a lady. The English soldiers would take her at her word and let her and her "maid" go. There were no women's clothes in the house large enough for Charles, who was rather tall, so the women servants in the MacDonald house were set to work to make an outfit for him. They sewed night and day and finally completed it.

At last Flora set out, taking the disguise with her, and was rowed across a narrow strait to the island of Benbecula, where she rendezvoused with the prince. When Charles had decked himself in the "Betty Burke" outfit, one of his followers burst out laughing. "They call Your Highness the Pretender," he said, eyeing Charles's large male feet, "but surely you are the worst of your kind!"

As Flora and the incognito prince crossed Benbecula to their embarkation point, by foot and by horse, everything went perfectly. They took a small boat and were ferried across the Sea of the Hebrides and landed safely on Skye. There, delivered into other loyal hands, the prince bade his benefactress good-bye and gave her, as a memento, the garters that "Betty Burke" had worn.

---

* Perhaps too fabulous. The very poor, among whom most Highlanders had to be classed, had difficulty perceiving the realness of large sums. If the government had offered ten pounds and a cow, Charles's fate might have been different.

Prince Charles ultimately escaped back to France, but Flora was not so lucky. The plot discovered (the boatman who had rowed the pair across the water had talked), she was arrested—along with other Highlanders known to have assisted the prince to escape—and taken to London. Her fellow conspirators were ruthlessly punished, 120 of them hanged. But Flora MacDonald's exploit had caught people's imagination, English as well as Scots, and the government did not quite dare proceed against her. After a year of imprisonment, during which she was neither tried nor charged with any crime, she was released. The people of the Highlands made her their heroine.

Now, married to Allan, son of MacDonald of Kingsburgh, she had come upon hard times, and like so many of her people, she and her husband had decided to move to North Carolina. With them they took three of their seven children—sons Alexander and James, daughter Anne MacLeod—a son-in-law, Alexander MacLeod, and eight indentured servants.

The Highland Settlement

The emigrant ships were small and had poor accommodations. The passengers slept in a long ward with a row of beds on each side. Each bed was

A heroine in Scotland for her help in saving Prince Charles Stuart, Flora MacDonald emigrated to North Carolina with her family in 1774. But the MacDonalds' Loyalism soon made them prefer to return to their Highland home.

the same size and slept four people, while the servants lay on the floor between. Meals consisted of oatmeal, potatoes, beef neck, and spoiled pork. The voyage took about two months, and Allan, Flora, and the rest were thankful when they sailed into the mouth of the Cape Fear River.

Twelve miles up the river was Brunswick, the port of entry. The MacDonalds saw a few scattered buildings on the edge of the woods—a tavern, a church, a customs house, a courthouse, a jail, and some stores. North and south of the town were plantations. The river was a busy place, with flatboats carrying grain, lumber, and barrels of salted meat to Wilmington. Other boats made their way upstream with sugar, rum, clothing, and manufactured items from England to be sold in Cross Creek and Campbelltown. Along the roads came wagons loaded with grain and droves of hogs or black cattle being driven to market.

Twenty miles upriver was Wilmington. The MacDonalds headed farther on, to the Cross Creek country, which though still part of the coastal plain, was far inland. This was the center of Highland settlement.

About twenty thousand Highlanders were living here when Flora and Allan arrived. Most of them were engaged in producing naval stores, but some farmed. Their houses by now were well furnished with chairs, beds, chests, blankets, tea services, china, and silver, and every home had bookshelves built into the living room.

Allan MacDonald bought 475 acres of land on Cheeks Creek in Anson County, of which seventy acres were already cleared. There was an orchard with peach and apple trees, a gristmill, dwelling house, barn, stable, and corn crib. Naming their new home Killigray, he and Flora settled down to live in peace and comfort.

But peace was no longer a way of life in North Carolina, as the MacDonalds soon learned. "The Troubles" had already begun. Every day they heard talk about "rebels," "Sons of Liberty," and "treason."

The Edenton Tea Party

From 1766, when the Stamp Act was repealed, to 1773, the excitement of defying Parliament had died down considerably. Only the committees of correspondence in the various colonies, writing encouragement to one another and keeping information flowing, maintained their original fervor. Then Parliament obligingly sparked off a new bonfire of revolt.

The Townshend duties on paper, painters' colors, glass, and tea, passed in 1767 as a kind of substitute revenue provider, had been reduced merely to a small import duty on tea. The colonists had managed to sustain a successful boycott of this pleasant beverage, but Parliament thought it knew a way to break that—and do a favor to the faltering East India Company at the same time, for the great importing firm had found

The English, as this cartoon shows, made much fun of the ladies of Edenton, whose formal avowal of support for the tea boycott is called the Edenton Tea Party. But today the ladies' action is widely hailed as a very early incursion of women into politics.

itself with a large overstock of tea. Parliament's idea was simple: Reduce the price of tea to a ridiculous amount, add the Townshend duty (which would still leave the tea selling for less than it sold for in England), and induce Americans to forget their silly objections to a tea tax.

It didn't work out quite that way.

The tea began to arrive late in 1773. New York and Philadelphia refused to let the tea ships dock. At Charleston, the tea was stored in damp cellars, where it lay rotting. In Boston, a group of citizens disguised as Indians boarded the tea ships and dumped the cargo into Boston Harbor. It is said that for days afterward every beach for miles around Boston was strewn with damp tea leaves.

North Carolina, not a big shipping colony, had less stake in this than some others. But a Brunswick merchant, William Hill, did write to his London agent to complain: For eleven months he had not been able to get any tea from them, and now that the *Sally* had finally arrived with his order, the local people would not let it be landed—poison would be more acceptable.

Parliament, indignant over the Boston Tea Party, decided to make an example of the city. The Boston Port Bill closed the port as of June, 1774, and moved the colonial capital to Salem. The Massachusetts committee of correspondence appealed to committees of correspondence in the other colonies, asking for help. North Carolinians agreed that the "cause of Boston is the cause of all." They immediately loaded the sloop *Penelope* with 2,096 bushels of corn, 22 barrels of flour, and 17 barrels of pork and sent it to Salem for the relief of Boston.

Fifty-one ladies from several counties wanted to demonstrate their patriotism in their own way. They held a meeting in Edenton at which they passed a resolution stating that they could not remain "indifferent to whatever affected the peace and happiness of the country." Then, in a solemn procession, they took all the tea from their kitchens, placed it in a pile, and burned it.

The news of this Edenton Tea Party caused much merriment among English opponents of the American position, who derided the ladies for thinking they understood that exclusively male province, politics. But many who agreed with the American colonies on the tax question commended the ladies of Edenton for their action. They were called "the patriotic ladies" and were described as "being typical of the attitude of the women in the colonies." Today the meeting is often noted as an extremely early example of women in politics.

The Last Colonial Assembly

Confident Governor Josiah Martin did not find things as easy as he had expected. John Ashe (the resist-to-blood-and-death man), who for many years had been colonel of the New Hanover County militia, refused to accept a new commission from Governor Martin. He preferred to be a colonel in the Patriot militia. Hugh Waddell of Wilmington, who had forced the Regulators to take the oath of allegiance for Governor Tryon, had also deserted the Parliament cause for that of the colonies.

The committees of correspondence continued to send couriers back and forth throughout the colonies with messages. It was decided that a congress should be held in Philadelphia, composed of delegates from each province, to discuss the common interests of all colonies. To elect delegates to this congress, the North Carolina assembly had to meet.

Governor Martin indignantly refused to call the assembly in time for them to elect the delegates. "Bold John" Harvey, speaker of the assembly, declared that it would meet without the governor's sanction. North Carolina's First Provincial Congress—the first anywhere in America to meet in defiance of English orders—convened August 25, 1774. It sat for only three days, but it launched the colony irrevocably into revolution. After passing a resolution criticizing Parliament and declaring its colonial tax illegal, the members elected William Hooper, Richard Caswell, and Joseph Hewes as delegates to the First Continental Congress (September 5 to October 26, 1774).

When Governor Martin called a meeting of the assembly the following spring, Speaker Harvey promptly summoned the Second Provincial Congress at the same place the day before, to elect delegates to the Second Continental Congress (May 10, 1775, to December 12, 1776). The colonial assembly consisted of nearly the same members as the Second Provincial Congress, and that body, meeting the following day, voted to approve the Continental Congress and endorsed its chosen delegates. Governor Martin grew so angry that he dissolved the group; this was the last royal assembly to be held in the colony of North Carolina.

The Mecklenburg Declaration of Independence

On April 19, 1775, war, whose long fuse had been touched off by the Boston Tea Party, finally reached the powder keg: Lexington and Concord. News of the battle was carried by couriers on horseback from one committee of correspondence to the next, down the coast. On May 3, the courier from Nansemond reached Edenton; on May 6, New Bern; two days later, Wilmington and Brunswick; on May 9, Hillsboro.

A meeting of the local Committee of Safety, a group recently organized by the Patriots to perform executive functions on the local level, was called in Mecklenburg County. In May, the delegates met at a tavern owned by an Irishman, Patrick Jack, and his son, James, a captain in the militia. On May 20, 1775, after two days of discussions, the committee drew up a list of resolutions remarkably similar to the later Declaration of Independence. They stated that anyone who invaded their rights was an enemy. They dissolved political connections with England, declared themselves a free and independent people, and acknowledged no commission, civil or military, issued by the Crown of Great Britain.

When the so-called Mecklenburg Declaration of Independence was completed, Captain James Jack was appointed to take it to Philadelphia, where the Second Continental Congress had just convened. Captain Jack set out on horseback and rode the forty miles to Salisbury that day. The declaration was read to the court there, and all but two members voted approval. When the Sons of Liberty in Charlotte heard this, ten or twelve of them saddled up their horses, rode to Salisbury, arrested the two dissenters, and took them to Charlotte for trial as traitors.

Captain Jack continued to Philadelphia, where he presented the Mecklenburg papers to Caswell, Hooper, and Hewes along with instructions from the committee that they be submitted to the Continental Congress. The North Carolina delegates, however, did not think the Congress was prepared to act on "absolute independence." They showed the declaration to John Hancock, John Jay, and Thomas Jefferson, and although the three agreed with the sentiment of patriotism, they still hoped for some form of reconciliation with England. No record of the Mecklenburg Declaration was made, nor was any vote taken on it by the Congress.

Captain Jack, finding his long journey in vain, said to the delegates: "Gentlemen, you may debate here about reconciliation—but bear in mind, Mecklenburg owes no allegiance to and is separated from the Crown of Great Britain."

Back in Charlotte a great crowd had gathered to hear the results of the committee meeting. Colonel Thomas Polk, the commanding officer of the county militia, read the declaration. The crowd broke into cheers and tossed their hats into the air. Unanimous applause ratified the independence of Mecklenburg County.

Within the next two weeks the Declaration was published in the *North Carolina Gazette*, the *Cape Fear Mercury*, and the newspaper in Charleston, South Carolina. Governor James Wright of Georgia mailed a copy to the colonial agent in England, and Governor Martin forwarded a copy of the *Cape Fear Mercury* with a long letter telling of the "Horrid" and "Treasonable" conditions.

The people of Mecklenburg, however, had had their say. With no more ado, they set about forming their own independent government, courts, and laws.

CHAPTER TWENTY

Choosing Up Sides

The events of early 1775 had greatly disturbed Josiah Martin—so much so that he had long since sent his family off to safety in New York. Proclamations against the Mecklenburg Declaration and other actions of the Patriots had won him exactly nothing. A request to General Gage for arms and ammunition with which to arm the Highlanders was intercepted by the Patriots. Rumors reached him daily that the Patriots planned to seize the palace and him in it, and when he planted some protective cannon in front of his palace, a drunken mob gaily carried most of them off.

Finally it all got to be too much for the frightened governor. Four days after the Mecklenburg Declaration, he spiked the few cannon that remained at the palace, hid the ammunition under the cabbages in his garden, locked the palace door, and fled to Fort Johnston at the mouth of the Cape Fear.

The Highlanders Decide

Meanwhile, all around him, men were deciding where they stood in this quarrel between the mother country and her colonies. They fell roughly into three groups—Whigs, moderates, and Tories.

About half the population were Whigs, or Patriots. Artisans, landholders large and small, they were spread over both coastal plain and Piedmont and even into the mountains. The Scotch-Irish—descendants of people who had fought valiantly for the Crown against Stuart adherents—were stout rebels almost to a man, but otherwise Patriot sentiment was spread over practically the whole colony.

The smallest group numerically was probably the moderates or "Neutrals." Some former Regulators belonged to this group, but the moderates obtained the bulk of their numbers from the Quakers and Moravians (pacifists) and the Germans, who preferred to sit out a quarrel they did not identify with.

The third group was the Tories or Loyalists. Merchants who had grown wealthy under the benign protection of the Royal Navy were its mainstay. Lawyers and professional men also tended to prefer the king's cause, as did those who held office by Crown appointment—customs officers, for example. But pen pushers would be of small use in the bloody conflict that now loomed. The people the embattled governor was hoping to win to the king's side were the Highland Scots of Cross Creek.

Since 1742, when the first kilted regiment, the Black Watch, had been mustered into the king's service, the British had been discovering that the wild Highlanders made first-class soldiers—hardy, disciplined, stoical, courageous to a fault. There was no reason to believe that the move to North Carolina had deprived them of this natural aptitude, so they were well worth having on one's side. Moreover, they were strongly motivated to prefer the status quo.

They held their lands directly from the Crown, and before they had left their native hills, a special oath of allegiance had been extracted from them—an oath that seemed particularly binding in this crisis. This close association with the Crown was extended to their principal occupation, production of naval stores, which was heavily subsidized by the government.

Furthermore, the side of interest was strengthened by the nature of these people. In 1745, they had been rebels, yes, but not rebels against the idea of kingship. They had merely wanted to replace one king with another—a medieval concept. Uneducated and primitive as many of them were, conservative by nature, accustomed to blind obedience to their chiefs, they found democracy unnatural and sinful. King George III was not the king they preferred, but he was better than no king at all.

Knowing all this, Governor Martin worked out a splendid scheme for reestablishing the royal authority in North Carolina by means of Highland troops recruited right in the colony. He wrote to Lord Dartmouth, the colonial secretary, outlining his idea: The government was to supply him with a force of regulars, which he would beef up with a unit of about seven thousand Loyalists, chiefly Highlanders. The regulars were to land in the Wilmington area and by their power and authority would soon overawe the impudent Patriots. Since the Patriot party still teetered on the edge of independence, not at all certain it wanted to topple over, perhaps this show of strength would induce it to pull back altogether. If worse came to worst, the Loyalists could use Wilmington as a base from which to conquer the province by force.

Before his messengers could return with Dartmouth's reply, however, Martin was told that local Patriots were about to attack Fort Johnston, his refuge. He abandoned the fort and fled to the British man-of-war *Cruizer*. Sure enough, the fugitive governor had hardly nipped out of the place before the Wilmington Committee of Safety attacked it and "wantonly in the dead hour of night set on fire and reduced to ashes the houses and buildings within the fort."

At this low point, Martin had a bit of good news. General Gage, the British commander-in-chief, had no troops to send him, but he could spare two experienced Highland officers—Lieutenant Colonel Donald MacDonald and Captain Donald MacLeod. They brought word that the government was offering generous bounties to all men who would enlist in the Royal Emigrant Highland Regiment—two hundred acres of land, remission of quit-rent arrears, and exemption from taxes for twenty years. Surely that would encourage recruiting if nothing else did!

Martin made MacDonald a brigadier general of militia and MacLeod a colonel, and sent them inland to recruit. With them went twenty-five other commissions to North Carolina settlers of known Loyalist leanings, empowering them to raise troops for the king's cause. Prominent among those receiving such commissions were Major Allan MacDonald, husband of Flora, his two sons, and his son-in-law.

Preparations

Leaving the military men to their recruiting, Governor Martin turned back to politics. On August 8, 1775, he issued the Fiery Proclamation, a document six feet long, which denounced the various committees that were running the colony and their "evil, pernicious and traiterous Councils and influence." Most people laughed at the intemperate language of this proclamation, but the Wilmington Committee of Safety (one of the "traiterous Councils" Martin was referring to) had the thing burned by the public hangman.

On August 25, the Third Provincial Congress met, denounced the Fiery Proclamation, established an elaborate form of interim local government, and authorized the raising of the regiments for the Continental Line and several units of militia.

The first job of these new troops was to help out Virginia, whose governor had been carrying out a fire-and-sword campaign against isolated plantations, and South Carolina, whose backcountry people had organized a Tory rising behind the lines. The North Carolinians were too late to help the Virginians, who delivered a bloody little defeat to a unit of regulars on December 9. But they offered timely aid to their sister state on December 22, defeating the Tories in a raging snow storm. By then it was time for North Carolinians to start worrying about problems in their own midst.

Throughout the fall the Highlanders had been busily recruiting. General MacDonald and Colonel MacLeod held meetings at houses throughout Cumberland and Anson counties, urging the men to enlist, explaining the

bounties and privileges that would be given to volunteers. Flora Mac-
Donald is said to have spoken at these meetings, using her name and influence to encourage other Highlanders to support the king's cause. And
support it they did, appearing at the recruiting camps in great numbers,
"in high spirits . . . well equipped with wagons and horses."

Not all Highlanders, especially those who had been settled in North
Carolina for a number of years, were altogether anxious to serve. They
knew it was no longer a matter of personal loyalty to a fatherlike sovereign
but a question of political philosophy and nationhood. Yet, because they
were of Highland blood, they hesitated to differ from their compatriots.

Farquhard Campbell, who had come to North Carolina in 1740 at the age
of nineteen, had already served on the Wilmington Committee of Safety as
a Patriot and had been appointed a delegate to all three of the provincial
congresses. But he found it hard to deny the pleas of his fellow Highlanders,
so he served on *both* sides. At one point during the war, he was imprisoned
as a Loyalist, but before the fighting was over, he had reverted to the
Patriot cause.

On January 3, Governor Martin heard from London, where Lord Dartmouth had been replaced by Lord George Germain. Despite the change in
ministry, the governor's plan had been approved—3,500 men were being
sent from Ireland under Charles Earl Cornwallis, another 2,000 under
Major General Henry Clinton. The governor straightway sent word to
Cross Creek for the Highlanders to assemble in Brunswick to be armed and
trained for their task.

Sometime before February 12, Flora MacDonald kissed her husband, sons,
and son-in-law good-bye and saw them off from Killigray. The three
MacDonalds and one MacLeod set out on horseback, leading two baggage
animals, while three gillies ran alongside, Highland fashion. In Cross Creek,
they rendezvoused with the rest of the newly raised Highland troops.

On February 18, they all set out for Brunswick—1,600 Highlanders in
bonnet and plaid, bagpipes skirling ancient battle tunes, drums beating
the step. A brave sight, but less formidable than it looked, for many of the
men were unarmed, and none had been trained. No matter. There was time
enough for that before the promised regulars arrived.

The Battle of Moore's Creek Bridge

Meanwhile, the Patriots knew perfectly well that something big was up.
But they had only 1,100 men and were thus seriously outnumbered by the
Loyalist force. Would it be better to wait awhile, augmenting their forces
until they were strong enough to match the Highlanders? Or assault them
now, before *they* had a chance to be reinforced? Brigadier General James

Moore, in command of the various Patriot units in the area, decided to act immediately.

The Moores had been important people in the Cape Fear region since 1713, when Colonel James, an uncle of the general, had marched to North Carolina's aid in the Tuscarora War. Maurice Moore, the general's brother —both were sons of the Maurice Moore who had settled in the valley in 1725—was an important colonial judge and had been so forthright a Patriot that Governor Tryon had tried to have him removed from the bench. Moore's Creek was named for the family.

Now the present James Moore, the general, thought that the creek, which flowed into the Black and thence into the Cape Fear, might be an excellent place to block the enemy's march. He would have to see that the Highlanders headed for Wilmington by this route.

Accordingly, he sent some of his meager forces to take Cross Creek in the Highlanders' rear, and other units to watch the fords of the Black and Cape Fear rivers. When the Highlanders managed to raise a sunken flatboat and use it to make a bridge over the Black, Moore ordered Colonels Richard Caswell and Alexander Lillington to march for Moore's Creek and to take and hold the bridge there.

While General Moore was at Rockfish Creek, he received a communication from General Donald MacDonald, the Highlanders' rather elderly commander. Moore and his men must obey the king and governor, he said, or be treated as enemies. Knowing that Caswell and Lillington had not yet had time to set up their defenses, Moore stalled. He would consult his officers, he replied to MacDonald.

Moore held off as long as he could, but at last he had to send MacDonald further word. He and his officers were in agreement, he said. "We consider ourselves engaged in a cause the most glorious and honorable in the world: the defense of the liberties of mankind." He enclosed a loyalty oath to the American cause, and said that if the Loyalists would just sign it, all would be forgiven them.

With that bland reply in his hand, Donald MacDonald knew that a battle was brewing. He called the Scots together and told them that if any man did not want to die for the cause, he could go home. Two companies of one battalion decided that they did not, after all, want to fight for the king of England, and twenty other men agreed with them and left. The remainder of the Highlanders resumed the march toward Brunswick.

Meanwhile, Farquhard Campbell, unable to make up his mind which cause he believed in, sneaked back and forth from one camp to the other. He told General MacDonald that Caswell and six hundred men were marching to join Moore. Later he informed Moore of the Highlanders' position.

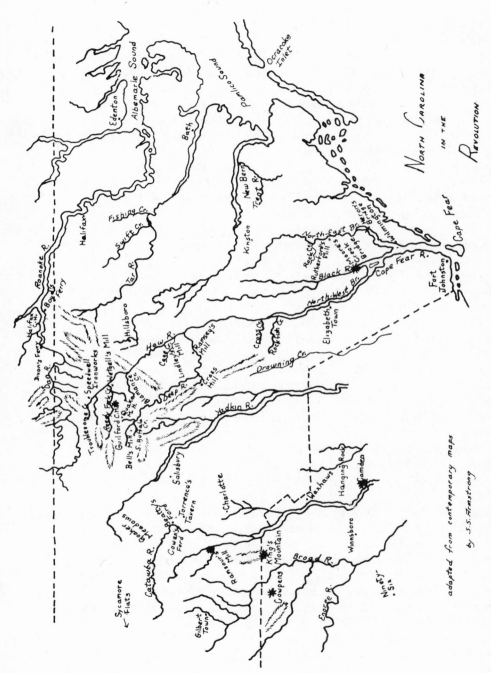

adapted from contemporary maps
by S. S. Armstrong

Only one major battle, Guilford Courthouse, was fought on North Carolina soil, but the state was the scene of innumerable small clashes between Loyalists and Patriots. In this well-watered country, it was usually a bridge or ford that men fought over.

As the Highlanders approached Moore's Creek, they had to march through difficult country filled with swamps and underbrush. Finally, before dawn on February 27, 1776, after a grueling all-night tramp, they paused for a council of war. Scouts told them that the Americans were up ahead, blocking their passage over the creek.

Caswell and Lillington had gotten there the night before.

The Americans, about one thousand strong, had also been up all night. On the west bank of the creek—the direction from which the Highlanders were marching—they had built some campfires and left them smoldering, to simulate an encampment. Then they had retired to the east bank, where they had built a hasty earthwork and mounted in it a pair of cannon. Known affectionately as Mother Covington and her daughter, the two heavy guns had been dragged through the forest with much labor. As a final touch to their preparations, Caswell's and Lillington's men had taken up the plank flooring of the bridge, leaving only the log sleepers, which they greased with tallow and soft soap.

The Highlanders, in their council of war, were in two minds about what to do. Seventy-year-old General Donald MacDonald, ill from exposure to the cold and rain, was put to bed in an improvised tent, while Colonel MacLeod and Major Allan MacDonald and other leaders talked with their scouts. The Americans' fake campfires had done their job, for the Highland scouts reported the Patriots camped on the west bank of the creek.

The younger officers wanted to attack immediately, but the older ones cautioned patience. The young men outvoted them, however, and although it was barely dawn of a raw, rainy day, they began to advance. Seventy-five picked men led the attack with claymores drawn. Slogging through the swamp, soaked kilts dragging around their legs, they came out at the bridge and found the still smoldering campfires.

Hardly pausing to note that the scouts had been duped, Colonel Donald MacLeod led the charge toward the bridge, shouting, "King George and broadswords!" The Highlanders stumbled after him.

A dim gray day had dawned, but the light hardly helped. After the first step or so, the charging Highlanders found nothing underfoot but a gaping hole and the slippery logs on either side. Skidding and lurching, they fell into the water or over one another and were too taken up with keeping their footing to use the few weapons they had. Colonel MacLeod and some others got across by jabbing the points of their swords into the wood, but as they reached the opposite bank, the Americans opened up with swan shot and cannon fire.

As MacLeod struggled up the slope toward the fortification, he was killed with "upwards of twenty balls through his body." Those who managed to

Few men were engaged, and the fighting lasted only three minutes, but the Battle of Moore's Creek Bridge was nonetheless a vital conflict. For the Patriot victory over Highland Loyalists staved off invasion of the South for three years.

follow him were either drowned or shot. In three minutes flat it was all over.

Driven back from the uncrossable bridge by withering fire, the Highlanders paused, uncertain. Major Allan MacDonald, to whom the command had fallen, ordered them to retreat up the creek to another crossing place and then to scatter to their homes.

But long before that could be accomplished, General Moore himself arrived and led the Americans in pursuit. They took 850 prisoners, including General Donald MacDonald, Major Allan, and the major's son Alexander. (James MacDonald escaped, and so apparently did Alexander MacLeod.) Loot included arms, wagons, and £15,000 in gold—all about equally valuable to the impoverished Patriots.

Mary Slocumb's Ride

This ruthless little battle was not without its human side as well as its official. Consider the story of Captain Ezekiel Slocumb of the Wayne County militia and his wife Mary.

When the Committee of Safety called out the Patriots to meet the High-landers, eighty men gathered at Captain Slocumb's home. As they left the house on Sunday morning, Mary watched in high spirits. That night she slept soundly and worked hard at her usual chores the following day. But she kept thinking where the men might be—how far they had marched and if they had met the Highlanders yet. When she went to bed that night, half-waking and half-dreaming, a vivid vision came to her. She saw a body wrapped in her husband's bloody guard coat and others dead and wounded on the ground. She screamed and sprang from the bed. Her only thought was that her husband needed her and she must go to him.

Dressing in haste, she went to the stable and saddled her mare, and in a moment was racing down the road at full speed. She knew the general route the little army expected to take, and she followed it without hesitation in the black night.

All night long she rode through the pine forests of Duplin and New Hanover counties. At sunrise, nearly seventy-five miles from home, she came on a group of women and children standing by the roadside and knew she was on the right road. She passed them without stopping, and in a few minutes she heard a sound like thunder, which she guessed to be the can-non. Then she could hear musketry. She turned her mare in the direction of the sounds, and under a clump of trees she saw about twenty wounded men lying on the ground.

A chill went through her, for it was the very scene she had seen in her dream.

Suddenly, as she looked around, she saw a body wrapped in her hus-band's bloody coat. She slid from the mare and ran across the remaining ground. When she stooped and uncovered the head, it was a bloody mass but still warm. A voice begged for water—a voice she did not know.

It was not Ezekiel Slocumb but a neighbor, whom her husband had wrapped in his own coat. A figure approached, and Mary looked up to see her husband, "as bloody as a butcher and as muddy as a ditcher." He had been chasing the Highlanders through the swamp after they retreated. Mary spent the remainder of the day helping tend the wounded on the battle-field.

Outcome

The battle of Moore's Creek Bridge was a kind of turning point in the Revolution. Politically speaking, it was an enormous help to the cause of independence.

North Carolinians who had hesitated and done much soul-searching over the idea of cutting loose from the protection of Great Britain now found the idea readily attractive. The timid, the indecisive, the doubtful were emboldened by the defeat of the redoubtable Highlanders. Those who naturally leaned toward whichever side looked like winning all at once found themselves ardent Patriots. It suddenly seemed both possible and desirable for Americans to separate from Great Britain.

For the Highlanders who had taken part in the conflict, it was another Culloden. Allan MacDonald and his fellow prisoners were forced to walk to Philadelphia, where they remained for eighteen months before being exchanged. Flora's servants deserted her, and many of her friends blamed Allan for their troubles. Straggling parties of plunderers stopped by Killigray almost daily, and she may at one time have been turned out of it. Once she was called before a provincial committee and questioned about some matter, to which she responded with pride and indignation. A friend wrote to her imprisoned husband: "I am happy to hear of Mrs. MacDonald's . . . Spirited behavior when brot before the Committee of Rascals."

More than two years after the battle, Alexander MacLeod arrived at Brunswick and took the members of his family, including his mother-in-law, to New York, where Flora was reunited with Allan. In the early fall of 1778, Allan was ordered to Halifax, Nova Scotia, to join the Highlanders there. That winter they moved on to Fort Edward at Windsor. The cold, damp weather kept Flora ill most of the time, and in October, 1779, Allan arranged for her to return to Scotland. Allan, too, returned to Skye after the war was over in 1783. Neither of them ever went back to North Carolina —two valiant people from another historical time, outmoded in a vigorous young colony about to become a state.

Major General Charles Earl Cornwallis commanded two invasion forces in the South. In the spring of 1776, his men ravaged two plantations, then returned to their ships and sailed away. But they would be back.

For the British Moore's Creek forced a change in plans out of all proportion to the number of men actually engaged in the scrap.

Early in April, the force promised to Governor Martin began to arrive —first Clinton, then the grand fleet of Sir Peter Parker, transporting Lord Cornwallis and the troops from Ireland. But now that the Highlanders had been scattered—and the Patriots, it was learned, had 9,400 men under arms, militia and Continentals—what was to happen to the governor's fine plan?

Martin decided to see what another proclamation would do. On May 5 he issued it, declaring North Carolina to be in a state of rebellion, ordering all congresses to be dissolved, and offering pardon to any rebel who would denounce the new government.

Two days passed. Not a single person came forward to accept the offer of pardon. Finally Clinton ordered Cornwallis to land and punish the two chief offenders within reach.

On May 12, Cornwallis landed with nine hundred men and set out for Orton Plantation (about fourteen miles from modern Wilmington), which had been settled originally by another uncle of General Moore. A force of Americans, about 150 men, had been stationed at Orton under a major, but they made no attempt to defend it. When the alarm was raised, they retreated hastily, abandoning baggage and provisions to the British. Cornwallis burned the Orton mill and marched on to the plantation of Brigadier General Robert Howe, another Patriot soldier. Seizing twenty bullocks there, he returned to the ships.

The little expedition had been a success as far as it went, but how far did it go? Burning a few plantations near the seashore wasn't the same as returning an entire province to its allegiance. Yet, without the large force of Loyalists that Martin had promised them, the British hesitated to attempt the conquest of all North Carolina.

With Cornwallis' troops back on board, Clinton gave the order to sail away. It would be 1779 before the British would return in force.

The little battle at Moore's Creek Bridge had turned out to be a brilliant strategic stroke, postponing the major British assault on the South for three crucial years.

CHAPTER TWENTY-ONE

A State Is Born

Everyone in North Carolina was now talking of independence. When the Fourth Provincial Congress met at Halifax in April, 1776, the delegates voted unanimously for the famous Halifax Resolves: "Resolved, that the delegates for this Colony in the Continental Congress be impowered to concur with the delegates of other Colonies in declaring Independency."

A copy of the Resolves was sent to Joseph Hewes, North Carolina representative in the Continental Congress. Newspapers throughout the colonies reprinted them and urged their representatives to follow the example of North Carolina.

Free and Independent

On May 15, 1776, the Virginia Provincial Congress instructed its delegates to formalize North Carolina's proposal. On June 7, in the Continental Congress, Richard Henry Lee of Virginia moved "that these United Colonies are and of right ought to be free and independent States. . . ." Congress adopted Lee's resolution on July 2, and two days later voted unanimously for approval of the final draft of the Declaration of Independence. William Hooper, Joseph Hewes, and John Penn signed for North Carolina.

William Hooper was born in Boston and was graduated from Harvard in 1760. Four years later he settled in Wilmington, where he gained a reputation as an active Patriot. Soon after he signed the Declaration of Independence, he resigned his seat in the Continental Congress and returned home to take part in local politics.

John Penn had succeeded Caswell as a delegate. He was born in Virginia, where he studied law. In 1774, he moved to Greenville County, North Carolina, and was elected a delegate to the Continental Congress when Caswell was made president of the Provincial Congress.

While Hooper and Penn went back and forth from Philadelphia to North Carolina, Joseph Hewes stayed in Philadelphia and worked for independence. He was a businessman and was more experienced in public affairs than the other two. He was connected with a mercantile house, and because he was associated with shipping, he was assigned to the Marine Committee of the Continental Congress, through which he handled the duties of secretary of the navy during the war. In a letter to a friend, he said that he worked some days from six in the morning until five or six in the afternoon without eating or drinking.

A copy of the Declaration of Independence did not arrive in North Carolina until July 22. The assembly was in session at Halifax at the time, and the delegates decided that it should be read in public on August 1, so that as many people as possible could come to hear it.

The county militia was drawn up in full array when at noon Cornelius Harnett (who went looking for the comptroller in Governor Tryon's house during the Stamp Act crisis), president of the Committee of Safety, stepped to the rostrum erected in front of the courthouse. Harnett raised his hand to hush the shouting crowd, then read the Declaration as solemnly as if it were a prayer. Cheers broke out again, and the militiamen placed Harnett on their shoulders and paraded him through the streets.

The next step was to form a permanent state government. It would not be a simple task. Settlement now spread for more than 350 miles, from New Bern to present Asheville. Moreover, although all those who were trying to draw up the constitution were Patriots, there was almost as much difference

William Hooper (above left), Joseph Hewes (above center), and John Penn (above right), signed the Declaration of Independence for North Carolina. A copy of the document reached the state July 22 and on August 1 was read in public to a cheering crowd.

of opinion among them as to what the new state government should be like as there was between Patriot and Loyalist.

The large landholders along the coast were conservatives who wanted a government of limited democracy, like the one under which they had lived when governed by England. The small farmers in the backcountry were liberals who believed that every man whether rich or poor, educated or ignorant, should have a voice in his government.

The Provincial Congress selected a committee to draft a constitution. The committee received suggestions from delegates of each county. Constitutions of Delaware, Rhode Island, Virginia, South Carolina, and New Jersey were examined. For three weeks the committee worked and haggled. Then, on December 6, 1776, Thomas Jones presented the council with a first draft. Copies were made for each county, and more discussion followed.

When the North Carolina constitution was finally adopted, it provided for a bicameral legislature, one body to be called the House and the other the Senate—a word introduced by Virginia for the first time in American history. Representatives to the House were to be elected by all those who had paid their public taxes. Senators were to be voted for only by "freemen," who possessed a freehold of fifty acres. The governor and other state officers were to be elected not by the people but by the legislature.

Both conservatives and liberals had to make concessions before the constitution was finally accepted. The document was not submitted to the people for approval but was simply adopted by the council. Richard Caswell was chosen to be governor of the state.

Frontier War

Meanwhile, war had started up again in the mountain settlements. In July, 1776, the Cherokee—enraged by incursions into their land, encouraged by British agents, and assisted by some Tories—launched a series of assaults up and down the southern frontier, from Georgia to Virginia. Isolated cabins were raided, men, women, and children slain, settlements burned. Scalps, stripped from the heads of the dying, could be sold to the British for so many pounds apiece. Those who escaped the initial surprise spent days, weeks, sometimes months penned up in crowded stockades, short of food and desperate.

All four colonies, which had been drilling militia in anticipation of using them against the British, were in a state of unusual preparedness for this kind of thing. Instead of stalling for months, while assemblies argued over the cost of arraying militia, all four sent expeditions against the Cherokee. Georgia's was small, Virginia's late, but the two Carolina campaigns were large, swift, brutal, and thorough.

In August, 1,100 South Carolinians under Colonel Andrew Williamson followed the same invasion route into Cherokee country that the two regular expeditions had followed in 1759 and 1761. A 2,400-man North Carolina force under Brigadier General Griffith Rutherford crossed the mountains at Swannanoa Gap (near modern Asheville) and attacked the most populous portion of the Cherokees' homeland. Joining up with Williamson, the North Carolinians proceeded to burn Cherokee houses, cut down Cherokee cornfields, uproot Cherokee gardens, and drive off the defenseless Cherokee women and children, whose men were off waging war on the whites.

Most Cherokee were ready to make peace by the time the Virginians belatedly arrived on the scene, and an agreement was patched up. But one fierce group, under an experienced warrior named Dragging Canoe, was more deeply embittered than ever by the whites' depredations. They moved to a new location along the Tennessee River (near modern Chattanooga), and from there they continued to raid the settlements as they chose.

Frontier warfare had not been stopped by these 1776 expeditions, but the brunt of it was deflected onto Kentucky—an over-mountain county of Virginia. Kentucky had been penetrated by white settlers in 1775 under the leadership of a forty-one-year-old long hunter named Daniel Boone. Boone, born near Reading, Pennsylvania, had moved with his family to present Davie County, North Carolina, in 1750, when he was sixteen. He more or less resided in the colony until 1769. Then, being a wilderness scout and explorer of great skill, he was hired to explore Kentucky for settlement and open up the mountain pass known as Cumberland Gap. In 1775, he led the first parties of settlers into the "dark and bloody ground," where they established three wilderness fort-villages: Boonesborough (near modern Ford, Kentucky), Harrodsburg, and Logan's Station (near modern Stanford, Kentucky). It was onto these settlements that the Cherokee—and sometimes their erstwhile enemies, the Shawnee—turned their full fury. Warfare was almost continuous until the 1790's.

And yet, despite the danger, these little towns held out and were even augmented by other wilderness stations. This emboldened one Richard Henderson, who had made a purchase of acreage to the south of them, to try to have his land settled. Previous claims of his had been disallowed by Virginia, but he was certain that this new claim lay south of Virginia's border and hence belonged to North Carolina.

New Settlement in the Wilderness

Henderson's holdings were in a bend of the Cumberland River known as French Lick, an area whose fertility and beauty were legendary among Kentuckians. Unfortunately, French Lick lay deep in Cherokee country, and the routes to it were roundabout and painfully difficult. A party could either slog its way overland through Kentucky or could take the river route: down the Tennessee River—through the modern states of Tennessee, Alabama, Tennessee again, and Kentucky—to the Ohio River, then up the curving Cumberland to the site.

Late in 1779, Henderson's settlers set out in two parties—a group of men overland, driving cattle, and a fleet of flatboats carrying women, children, and household goods by the water route. Despite one of the coldest winters in American history, the first party made it to French Lick with only minor losses. The second party ran into trouble.

They were held up at first by the cold weather; it was late February, 1780, before the Tennessee River was navigable. The party pushed off at last from the region that is now northeastern Tennessee, rode the river safely as far as the Chattanooga area, and then found itself in danger. Here the river flowed swiftly through narrow gorges, forming whirlpools and foaming past jagged rocks—a navigational nightmare for the clumsy flatboats. The clever Dragging Canoe had chosen this as the best spot for an ambush.

First the rear flatboat was picked off, with a loss of nearly thirty persons. Then, as a canoe overturned and the whites went to the rescue, the Cherokee turned their fire on them. Four persons were hit, but a young girl in the rescue vessel seized the tiller and safely steered them clear. A third boat caught in some rocks, and the warriors gathered there. While one man held them off with a rifle, the others frantically dumped bundles overboard to lighten their vessel until it floated clear.

For an entire week, until the river had carried the party out of Dragging Canoe's country, the Indians kept up this sniping and assaulting. The settlers reached the Ohio on March 20 and then began the laborious job of poling the flatboats up the Cumberland. At last, on April 24, this second party reached French Lick and rejoined their waiting kin.

By then the settlers had had certain word that French Lick was part of North Carolina, not of Virginia. They celebrated by writing and signing an ordinance of self-government and by naming their new settlement Nashborough, in honor of Brigadier General Francis Nash, a North Carolina soldier who had fallen at Germantown.

Nashborough was the most exposed settlement in North America and remained so throughout the Revolution. Its first stockade had hardly been erected before it was under Indian attack, and these assaults and raids continued without letup through the Revolution and far beyond. Peace did not come to French Lick until the entire frontier was pacified in 1794. But Nashborough held out. Its people were determined to make something permanent of their settlement.

In November, 1789, North Carolina ratified the United States Constitution and became the twelfth state of the Union. Here is the original seal of the eight Lords Proprietors (left) side by side with the official state seal (right). The obverse sides of both seals are shown here.

In 1784, the North Carolina legislature decided it didn't like the English sound of Nashborough and preferred to honor France, America's new ally, by renaming the town Nashville. In 1790, North Carolina ceded its overmountain territory to the new United States, and six years later the region was admitted to the union as the sixteenth state—by name, Tennessee.

By that time, little Rachel Donelson, who had made the terrible flatboat journey to French Lick in 1780, had grown up and married a young North Carolina lawyer and soldier. Mrs. Andrew Jackson died in 1828; if she had lived a few more months, she would have become America's seventh First Lady.

CHAPTER TWENTY-TWO

The War in the South

Meanwhile, in North Carolina proper, no military operations took place between 1776 and 1780. There was activity aplenty, however, for troops were raised, organized, equipped, trained, and maintained. Men, money, and supplies were sent to other states to aid in fighting there, serving under General Washington in New York, Pennsylvania, and New Jersey. Hundreds of North Carolinians endured the hardships at Valley Forge during the harsh winter of 1777–78.

In 1779, finding that the northern campaign had won them nothing but battles, the British decided to try the South again. Still convinced that there was a Mother Lode of Loyalist sentiment floating around if only they could locate and mine it, they launched an attack on Savannah, Georgia. Robert Howe, who had been promoted and was now a major general, was ordered to do what he could to protect the city.* He had only seven hundred Continentals, some Georgia militia, and a large swamp to work with. When the British found a way through the swamp, Howe was bloodily defeated. With a remnant of his command, he retreated across the river into South Carolina.

For this defeat, Howe, North Carolina's highest military officer during the war, was court-martialed and dismissed, and Major General Benjamin Lincoln was assigned to command in the South. Throughout 1779, this fight seesawed along the Georgia–South Carolina border. But in the end Lincoln did not do even as well as Howe, who had at least saved some of his command. When Clinton and Cornwallis arrived, February 11, 1780, to assault Charleston, Lincoln took a large Continental force into the city. On May 12, he was forced to surrender both Charleston and troops. Included among the prisoners of war were 815 North Carolina Continentals and about 600 militia.

* This promotion would probably have gone to James Moore, but in April, 1777, General Moore died in Wilmington. By coincidence, his brother the judge died in the same house on the same day.

After the fall of Charleston, Clinton returned to New York and left Lord Cornwallis in command of the southern campaign. For the moment, there was nothing for the energetic earl to do. Georgia and South Carolina were prostrate, and the subjugation of North Carolina could wait until fall, when the maturing crops would make it easier to keep horses and men fed. He reestablished royal rule in South Carolina and settled down to wait for harvest.

Early in 1780 Charleston was laid under siege by Major General Sir Henry Clinton (left) and on May 12, it surrendered—a major military disaster for the Americans. From fallen Charleston, the British rapidly advanced inland.

Guerrilla Warfare

What Cornwallis had not counted on was such men as Francis Marion, Andrew Pickens, and Thomas Sumter in South Carolina, and Griffith Rutherford, William R. Davie, William Lee Davidson, and Francis Locke in North Carolina. These men did not wait for harvests or formal campaigns. They simply launched guerrilla war—sudden midnight attacks on an encampment of soldiers, hand-to-hand combat with an isolated patrol, hit-and-run ambush on a file of dragoons. In particular, they made war on the Loyalists and their troops, burning and slaughtering and marauding—and often out of personal vendetta as much as political conviction. It was cruel and ruthless warfare, largely American against American.

No longer confined to the coastal plain, this brand of fighting quickly spread into the Piedmont and the mountains. Early in June, 1780, Colonel John Moore, a Loyalist who lived near Ramsour's Mill in Lincoln County, got tired of waiting for Cornwallis to "liberate" North Carolina. He assembled about 1,300 Tory troops. On June 20, a Patriot force of about 400 North Carolina militia, under the command of Colonel Francis Locke, approached the mill. At daybreak they attacked, and although the Tories had an excellent position and outnumbered them by more than three to one, Colonel Locke's forces managed to outflank and catch the Tories in a crossfire. Soon the Loyalists broke and began to run. Some did not stop until they had reached the British camp at Camden.

None of the men on either side wore uniforms of any kind, and as they came together in battle it was hard to tell who was on which side. One soldier said later that relatives and good friends fought on opposite sides, and when the smoke cleared, they would recognize one another even as they shot.

The Loyalist scouts kept Cornwallis well informed of such skirmishes, and although the Loyalists were impatient for action, he told them to work their crops and keep quiet until the English troops entered North Carolina. The earl was contemptuous of all American troops, especially the state militias. They had no uniforms, few guns, and little ammunition. To his mind, they were "rabble" who had no respect for the formal, gentlemanly rules of warfare. When he was ready to march through North Carolina, which he scornfully called "the road to Virginia," they would either join him or run. Meanwhile, the ungentlemanly attacks of the Patriot bands made it almost impossible for his supply troops to forage for food.

In late July, William Davie and his small cavalry troop were near Hanging Rock, where Cornwallis had established an outpost. They watched as a convoy with provisions made its way slowly along the forest road. Then Davie raised his hand, and the Patriots swooped down on the supply wagons before the enemy knew they were near. Dragoons and Loyalists guarding the convoy were captured, horses and guns taken. But the wagons of provisions, too cumbersome to be carried off at the guerrillas' swift pace, were burned.

A few days later, Davie and his men reappeared at Hanging Rock. Three companies of mounted infantry were just returning from an expedition. Within view of the garrison, the Patriots attacked. Under the circumstances, they could not carry off human prisoners, but they took one hundred muskets and sixty horses without losing a single man.

With Colonel Sumter of South Carolina, Davie now planned a combined attack on Hanging Rock. Sumter was fresh from a failed attempt to seize a Loyalist fort on the hills above the Catawba River, but the two Patriot leaders had about 800 men between them and felt confident. Hanging Rock too was held by Loyalist troops, and the resistance was stiff. At last the Patriots succeeded in routing the enemy. While the victors were plundering the camp and getting drunk, however, the Loyalists rallied and returned to the fray, this time holding out until reinforcements came. This skirmish was one of the most bitterly fought battles in the entire war.

Disaster at Camden

Meanwhile, Benjamin Lincoln's successor, Major General Horatio Gates, had decided to attack the British troops at Camden. Gates had a large, ill-assorted, horribly ill-equipped force consisting chiefly of militia units from North Carolina and Virginia. Instead of marching these troops to Camden roundabout, which would have taken him through a friendly region where food was abundant, he chose the shorter road—through country both hostile and barren. His starving men, meagerly fed on green corn and molasses, were afflicted with what has been delicately called "loose bowels"; many of them could scarcely walk, let alone fight. Nevertheless, as they neared the British encampment, Gates ordered a night march, in hopes of surprising the enemy at dawn.

As luck would have it, Cornwallis, who had hurried up from Charleston with reinforcements for Camden, had decided on a night march, too. The two armies collided about two o'clock on the morning of August 16, 1780.

Skirmishing in the dark, they did little damage to one another. In the morning, however, when the ill-prepared Americans were attacked by the cavalry and bayonets of their well-drilled foes, most of them broke immediately and fled, none more precipitately than the North Carolina militia.

General Gates and General Caswell, who commanded these troops, tried to rally their men. Finding it impossible, they too left in hot haste, abandoning troops and supplies. A few miles from the battlefield, General Gates met Colonel Davie bringing reinforcements. He told Davie of the disastrous defeat, and Davie suggested that they return and bury the dead.

153

In August, 1780, exhausted and ill-fed Patriot forces were quickly overwhelmed at Camden, South Carolina, by Lord Cornwallis. With the Patriot general in flight and his troops scattered, North Carolina lay open to invasion.

"Let the dead bury their dead!" shouted Gates (a quotation from Matthew 8:22) and spurred his horse away.

Gates and Caswell reached Charlotte, seventy-eight miles from the battlefield, by eleven o'clock that night. Caswell remained in Charlotte to gather the militia, but Gates did not stop until he reached Hillsboro, 130 miles farther on.

In derision, Loyalist wits published a notice:

> STRAYED, DESERTED, OR STOLEN, from the subscriber, on the 16th of August last, near Camden, in the State of South Carolina, a whole ARMY, consisting of horse, foot and dragoons, to the amount of near TEN THOUSAND. . . . The subscriber has very strong suspicions, from information received from his aid de camp, that a certain CHARLES, EARL CORNWALLIS, was principally concerned. . . .
>
> HORATIO GATES, M.G.

Cornwallis in North Carolina

With a victory—perhaps "rout" is a better word—like Camden under his belt, Cornwallis decided that it was time to move into North Carolina. He therefore divided his forces into three parts, which were to take separate routes and to meet in Charlotte.

The main unit he commanded himself. A second unit of one thousand Loyalists, mostly Scots, under the command of a regular army officer, Major Patrick Ferguson, was sent on a sweep to the west. It was hoped that its example would encourage enlistment among Tory-leaning peoples of the Piedmont.

The third unit consisted of one of the most famous fighting corps in the army—the British Legion, a cavalry corps under the ruthless leadership of twenty-six-year-old Colonel Banastre Tarleton. He was widely and justly feared. At the Waxhaws on the border between the Carolinas, the previous May 29, "Bloody Ban" had led his men in a spectacular assault on a Virginia unit, which had been quickly overwhelmed. Despite the fact that these Patriots had thrown down their arms and were trying to surrender, he allowed his men to saber them mercilessly. Henceforth, to Americans "Tarleton's quarter" meant no quarter at all.

Although harassed by Colonel Davie along the route, Tarleton was the first to reach Charlotte. From all over the state Patriots gathered, putting themselves under Davie's command. Determined not to let Bloody Ban enter the town peacefully, Colonel Davie posted his forces at the courthouse. On the morning of September 26, 1780, Tarleton's men were seen advancing. At sight of the Patriots, the colonel ordered his bugler to sound the charge, and the British Legion launched itself at the waiting Americans. Three times Tarleton charged, and each time the Patriots held their ground. The fourth time, Tarleton's infantry broke around Davie's flank, and the American leader withdrew his forces, each company covering the other, until they were out of danger.

Tarleton followed cautiously and charged the rear guard. They resisted stubbornly, but St. George Locke, son of General Locke, was literally cut to pieces by Tarleton's dragoons, and another officer left for dead was found with three bullet wounds and six saber cuts. The following day Davie joined Gates and the army at Salisbury, and Cornwallis established himself at Charlotte.

Cornwallis' army had to live off the country around it now. Charlotte made a good location for this, because the region had many grist mills where corn and wheat could be ground for the troops. But collecting the grain proved harder than the Englishman had anticipated. Cornwallis posted fifty men at Polk's Mill, two miles from Charlotte, but sixty American cavalrymen made a long loop around Charlotte and attacked the mill. They were repulsed, eventually, but not without a fight.

Five days later Cornwallis sent a detachment to forage for supplies in the fertile fields of Long Creek, about ten miles northwest of Charlotte. When 110 wagons stopped at one farm, a local Patriot officer hastily rounded up thirteen of his neighbors and attacked the English, killing eight and

155

wounding twelve. Such assaults could be easily repulsed, of course, whenever Cornwallis wished, but the need to expect them and prepare a defense was nerve-wracking in itself, a constant harassment to the king's forces.

Kings Mountain

With him Cornwallis had brought the former governor, Josiah Martin, who still believed the Loyalists would flock to his side if they had a chance. Once again he resorted to his favorite device and issued a proclamation. This one promised full pay and free grants of land at the end of the war to anyone who would join him.

Martin sent the notice by couriers to the coast and into the backcountry, but before it could have any effect, the news arrived that Cornwallis' second unit, Major Patrick Ferguson and his corps of Scots Loyalists, had been wiped out on October 7.

Caught at Kings Mountain, just across the border in South Carolina, the Loyalists had been surrounded by a number of independent companies of backcountrymen—mostly Scotch-Irish, so that Kings Mountain became, in effect, Scots against Scots—and to a man the Loyalists were either killed or captured. In the hard bitterness of the times, the victors hanged a number of their prisoners for previous maraudings.

So closely surrounded was General Cornwallis by local Patriots that news of this calamity did not reach him for a full week. Nor could he get reliable reports on what was going on back in the South Carolina he had left. He certainly wasn't doing his cause much good in Charlotte. Instead of the Loyalists flocking to his standard, as Governor Martin had promised, he had found North Carolina "a damned hornet's nest." On October 12, as the rainy season set in, he abandoned Charlotte and returned to South Carolina, making camp at Winnsboro.

He did not know it, but Loyalist support for the British had already peaked. From Kings Mountain on, enthusiasm for the king's cause faded.

CHAPTER TWENTY-THREE

In October, 1780, George Washington chose a replacement for Horatio Gates as commander-in-chief in the South: Major General Nathanael Greene of Rhode Island. Good-looking, quick-witted, well-read in military matters, Greene had been an anchor smith and ironmaster in civil life and a Quaker by religion. His fascination with military matters and weekly drilling with the local militia had gotten him read out of meeting, but it had also brought him to the notice of the authorities at the time when Americans were mobilizing. As a result, Greene received what must surely be the most dizzying promotion in military history—from private in the militia to brigadier general of Continentals.

When Greene arrived in Charlotte in December, 1780, the forces under his command consisted of about two thousand ragged, starving scarecrows. His first problem, he decided, was to get these men fed. South Carolina had more food than North just then, so, like Cornwallis before him, he divided his army. He sent Brigadier General Daniel Morgan, a Virginia veteran of long and distinguished experience, with a small force of Continentals and North Carolina militia westward in the direction of Greenville, while he himself took the main body of troops eastward toward Cheraw. This left Cornwallis between them—a traditional military blunder.

Cornwallis evidently subscribed to the tradition, for he gleefully sent Colonel Tarleton after Morgan with about one thousand men. Bloody Ban caught up with the Virginian near the Broad River (modern Chesnee, South Carolina), where Morgan was awaiting him on a rising patch of ground. The area, which had been used as a roundup center by the region's cattlemen, was called the Cowpens.

It was dawn, January 16, 1781. Tarleton, overconfident, attacked precipitately, expecting to set the North Carolina militia running like rabbits. But Morgan understood militia and had instructed them carefully. They gave way before the legion's assault, then ran around behind the hill, re-formed, and returned to fight again. The unwary dragoons soon found themselves surrounded and prisoners.

The Cowpens, a brilliant battle, marked another turning point for the British. Tarleton himself had escaped with about twenty of his dragoons, but the legend of his invincibility died in the battle. After Cowpens, Patriots still hated Tarleton, but they no longer regarded him with superstitious fear.

Race Across North Carolina

Lord Cornwallis was taken aback by the news of Tarleton's unexpected defeat—"The late affair has almost broke my heart," he wrote to a friend. But not being one to sit around wringing his hands, he immediately burned his cumbersome baggage, except for ammunition wagons, and set out in pursuit of Morgan, eager to bring the rebels to a major battle. His best hope of doing this was by pinning them against one of the major rivers that crossed the Piedmont—the Catawba, the Yadkin, the Deep, and the Dan—rivers now in flood and sometimes unfordable.

At Guilford Courthouse, after Greene had galloped 125 miles in three days, Morgan and Greene were reunited. Relieved of the load of prisoners Morgan had been herding since Cowpens, they marched out, heading north. They knew Cornwallis was after them, and being wholly unprepared for battle, they were as anxious to escape him as he was to capture them. It became a race across North Carolina to the Dan River. Once they had crossed that stream, which roughly marked the Virginia border, they would be safe.

But a long road still separated them from their goal—a long road and several major rivers.

The waters of the Yadkin River were already rising when the Americans arrived at Trading Ford on February 1. A fleet of small boats was waiting for them, and the troops lost no time crossing. When Cornwallis reached the river two days later, it was too swollen to ford, and no boats were to be had. The earl ordered his gunners to bombard the American camp across the river, but the cannonballs did little damage. One actually hit the roof of Greene's headquarters causing the shingles to fly, but Greene, inside writing his report, merely blotted his paper and went on writing.

On and on went this frantic race. On February 10, General Morgan, crippled by arthritis and ague, had to give up and go home. The Patriots who remained trudged along wet clay roads, which froze hard at night and turned into slippery mud in the day. Hundreds of the soldiers had no shoes, and blood from their half-frozen feet marked the track of their passing. Tents, long since worn out, were abandoned and the men huddled together by the campfires at night—one blanket to four men—or built crude shelters of boughs to keep from freezing. Once a day they ate bacon and cornmeal.

Greene had no better comforts than his men. One night he and John Rutledge, the South Carolina governor, found an empty shed with some hay in it—compared to a leaky lean-to of boughs, a veritable palace. They fell exhausted on the hay and were soon sound asleep. But during the night they were awakened, each accusing the other of kicking him. The kicking continued, and when they pushed the hay to one side, they found that a large hog was sharing their bed.

Cornwallis doggedly followed Greene, mile after mile. Sometimes the two forces were so close together that anyone seeing them pass would have thought them to be one army, and occasionally Tarleton would rush forward to skirmish briefly with Colonel Otho Holland Williams, Greene's rear guard. Most of the time, however, all the energy of both armies was required simply to march.

At last, on February 13, the Dan loomed ahead of the exhausted Americans. A detachment was sent ahead to collect boats, and as the Patriots drew near the river, Greene ordered Colonel Williams to delay the pursuit as long as possible, in order to give the main body time to cross. Williams maneuvered his rear-guard company so skillfully that British scouts took it for the entire army, and Cornwallis prepared for battle. About three o'clock in the afternoon, Williams received word that Greene and the army had successfully crossed the Dan. A shout went up, and the rear guard, their job finished, took to the boats. By nine o'clock that night the last Americans were being rowed across the river while the horses swam.

General Charles O'Hara, who led the English advance corps, heard the joyous shout and guessed what it meant. He reached the bank of the Dan just in time to see the last Americans disappear on the other side.

A Costly Victory

Cornwallis was baffled. Technically he controlled Georgia, South Carolina, and North Carolina, and yet he still lay at a disadvantage. Having burned his provisions along with his other baggage, he now found his troops on short commons. Moreover, they seemed to have no allies among the populace.

The earl returned to Hillsboro, his supply base, to recoup. While he was there, he decided to make one last attempt to encourage the Tories to join him. He erected the king's standard with great pomp and ceremony, saluting it with twenty-one guns. Still with the army, Josiah Martin, one of history's great proclaimers, issued yet one more document, calling on the Loyalists to rally to the king's colors.

But the fate of a unit of Loyalists who tried to do so impressed the populace far more than proclamations and standards. The troops, under Dr.

John Pyle, expecting an escort from Tarleton's green-jacketed dragoons, were delighted when they saw green-clad horsemen approaching them. But it was not Tarleton—it was Light Horse Harry Lee, with a Patriot patrol, and he practically annihilated them all.

Cornwallis wrote later that many Loyalists rode up to his headquarters, shook his hand, and told him they were glad he was in North Carolina. But then they rode off again.

In Virginia, General Greene was having better luck. Three days after Cornwallis established himself at Hillsboro, the Americans, reinforced by Virginia militia and Continentals, recrossed the Dan and joined a troop of South Carolina horsemen under General Andrew Pickens near Guilford Courthouse. The Patriots numbered more than four thousand men while Cornwallis had only about half that many. Greene decided it was time to fight.

On March 14, 1781, hearing that Cornwallis was heading to meet him, Greene prepared for battle. He placed the North Carolina militia on both sides of the road to New Garden behind rail fences, with reinforcements in a woods about three hundred yards distant.

The following morning the Battle of Guilford Courthouse was fought. The English were within forty yards of the American troops before they saw them and charged with bayonets. The armies clashed, and the fighting was so fierce it was impossible to determine who was winning. When the Americans seemed on the verge of breaking through the British lines, Cornwallis ordered his gunners to fire grapeshot into the thickest fighting to drive them back. This killed many of his own men, but it also stopped the American charge.

For two hours the battle raged. Finally, his ammunition running low, Greene ordered a retreat, leaving Cornwallis the victor of the field. It was a Pyrrhic victory, however, like Bunker Hill. One fourth of the British soldiers were casualties, and a few days after the battle, Greene taunted the victor with the remark that he would be glad to sell him another American field at the same price.

The Americans were far from discouraged by Guilford. Their reaction to the battle was well expressed by a young Quaker farmer named William Armfield, who lived nearby. Armfield was angry at Cornwallis for having raided his fields for forage, and when he heard that the British were near, he took his squirrel gun one morning and announced that he was going hunting.

Although it was contrary to his Quaker beliefs, he joined the Patriot forces at Guilford Courthouse and fought with them the day of the battle. Unhurt, he returned home that evening. When his wife asked where was the game he had shot, Armfield replied, "It wasn't worth bringing home."

Chaos in the Wake of War

Cornwallis slowly made his way to Wilmington with his battered army. By then the earl had come to the conclusion that he was getting nowhere in the Carolinas and that the proper place to carry on the war was Virginia. Accordingly, about the end of April, he re-formed his now rested soldiers and set out northward, to the fate that awaited him in Yorktown. He left Governor Josiah Martin to run North Carolina—if "run" is the proper word.

Nathanael Greene also rested his men for a week and then abandoned North Carolina. Instead of pursuing Cornwallis, he turned toward South Carolina to reduce the British strongholds that remained there. By mid-September, nine months after he assumed command, the British were bottled up in Charleston and Savannah, and the rest of the colony was in Patriot hands.

North Carolina was not so lucky. Although the Piedmont, where earlier fighting took place, was now relatively quiet, the Cape Fear valley erupted. With the Patriot militia disbanded or serving with Greene, the Loyalists finally had control of the valley. They raided and plundered Patriots' houses and farms, stole their cattle, drove off their horses. Rebel leaders dared not sleep at home for fear of being captured at night. Whole districts turned entirely lawless, descending to a kind of warfare that was little better than family feuding.

The region near Elizabethtown, in the Highlanders' country, was a Tory stronghold, where men openly declared for the king. On August 11, four of their leaders rendezvoused at Cross Creek with their followers and launched a widespread raid on the surrounding countryside, taking prisoners and looting.

Patriots who had been forced to flee from their homes gathered in the Bladen area, 150 strong, and in the early morning of August 29 they attacked Elizabethtown. The surprised Tories were trapped, several of them killed. The remainder fled, many taking refuge in a deep ravine where the vengeful rebels could not find them. Since then this ravine has been named the Tory Hole.

Governor Burke, the Patriots' chief executive, tried to rally resistance around himself at Hillsboro. When word of this reached Wilmington, a local Tory militia leader sent troops to seize him. Burke was taken prisoner in September. The Patriots attempted to release him, but their ambush failed and he was safely delivered to Wilmington. The Loyalists imprisoned him on an island near Charleston, out of harm's way.

But the Patriots were aroused now, and men began to rally around General Griffith Rutherford. Captured in an earlier fray, Rutherford had been exchanged just in time to provide a focal point for reestablishing rebel control of the Cape Fear region.

With a respectable troop under his command, he set out to harass Wilmington by cutting off its supplies from the north. On November 17, he was encamped there, beginning to tighten his noose, when cavalryman Light Horse Harry Lee arrived from Virginia with news.

At Yorktown, the previous October 19, 1781, Lord Cornwallis had surrendered the entire force under his command. The war in the South was over.

Rutherford drew up his little army, and with peal after peal of musketry, they saluted the glad tidings. The Loyalists in Wilmington must have heard this *feu de joie*, for the next morning the British troops and poor old Governor Martin boarded ships and sailed away from North Carolina for good.

Sovereign State

The Revolution left animosities behind, of course, but if there was one thing citizens of the Old North State were used to, it was animosities. They'd lived through enough of them in their 120-year history—proprietorial party against antiproprietorial, Quaker against Anglican, Indian against white, pirate against sea keeper, Regulator against poll taxer, Loyalist against Patriot. Conflict was an old story in North Carolina, and the bitterness had never lasted for long. In time men would forget they were Huguenots or Moravians or Baptists, Highland Scots making naval stores, ex-indentured servants turned rich planters, Scotch-Irish of the backcountry, Germans placidly tending their rich farms, Negroes free and slave. They would remember only that they were North Carolinians with a common heritage.

In November, 1789, a constitutional convention met at Fayetteville (formerly Cross Creek) and ratified the United States Constitution, making North Carolina the twelfth state of the union. Already abuilding was a little settlement in Wake County that was to be the "fixed and unalterable seat of government" for a sovereign state.

Men had no trouble choosing a name for their new capital. Whose dream had brought the first colonists to Carolina's shores? Whose time and energy and fortune had been spent to create an English-speaking nation in the New World? North Carolina was grateful to Washington and the other heroes for giving her freedom, but she wanted to honor first the man who had given her existence.

The new capital was named Raleigh.

Bibliography

Agniel, Lucien, *The Late Affair Has Almost Broke My Heart: The American Revolution in the South*. Riverside, Conn.: The Chatham Press, 1972.

Andrews, Charles M., *The Colonial Period of American History*. New Haven, Conn.: Yale University Press, 1937.

Arnett, Alex Mathews, and Jackson, Walter Clinton, *The Story of North Carolina*. Chapel Hill, N.C.: University of North Carolina Press, 1933.

Ashe, Samuel A., *History of North Carolina*. Greensboro, N.C.: Charles L. Van Noppen, Publisher, 1908.

Becker, Carl, *The Declaration of Independence*. New York: Alfred A. Knopf, 1953.

Bleeker, Sonia, *The Cherokees: Indians of the Mountains*. New York: William Morrow and Company, 1952.

Brandon, William, *The Last Americans*. New York: McGraw-Hill Book Co., 1974.

Brown, Douglas Summers, *The Catawba Indians*. Columbia, S.C.: University of South Carolina Press, 1966.

Camp, Cordelia, and Wilson, Eddie W., *The Settlement of North Carolina*. Durham, N.C.: Cordelia Camp, Publisher, 1942.

Colonial Dames of America in the State of Ohio, *North Carolina*. Cincinnati: The Ebbert and Richardson Co., 1927.

Commager, Henry Steele, and Morris, Richard B., eds., *The Spirit of 'Seventy-Six*. 2 vols. Indianapolis, Ind.: The Bobbs-Merrill Company, 1958.

Connor, R. D. W., *History of North Carolina*. Chicago: Lewis Publishing Company, 1919.

——— *The Old North State*. Philadelphia: J. B. Lippincott Company, 1906.

——— *Revolutionary Leaders of North Carolina*. Spartanburg, S.C.: The Reprint Company, 1971.

Craven, Wesley Frank, *The Colonies in Transition*. The New American Nation Series. New York: Harper & Row, 1968.

Duke, James B., *A History of the American Revolution*. New York: Alfred A. Knopf, 1969.

Fitch, William Edward, "The First Founders of America." A paper read at a meeting of the New York Society of the Order of the Founders and Patriots of America, October 29, 1913.

Foreman, Grant, *The Five Civilized Tribes*. Norman, Okla.: University of Oklahoma Press, 1934.

Grange, R. M. D., *A Short History of the Scottish Dress*. New York: The Macmillan Company, 1966.

Hawks, Francis L., *History of North Carolina*. Fayetteville, N.C.: E. J. Hale and Son, 1858.

Hodge, Frederick Webb, *Handbook of American Indians North of Mexico*. New York: Pageant Books Inc., 1959.

Hyde, George E. *Indians of the Woodlands*. Norman, Okla.: University of Oklahoma Press, 1962.

Johnson, F. Roy, *The Tuscaroras*. A Carolina Heritage Book. Murfreesboro, N.C.: Johnson Publishing Company, 1967.

Jones, John Seawall, *Defence of the Revolutionary History of the State of North Carolina*. Raleigh, N.C.: Turner and Hughes, 1834.

Kilpatrick, Jack Frederick, and Gritts, Anna, *Run Toward the Nightland*. Dallas: Southern Methodist University Press, 1967.

Lawson, John, *A New Voyage to Carolina*. Raleigh, N.C.: Strother and Marcom, 1860.

Lefler, Hugh T., *History of North Carolina*, 4 vols. New York: Lewis Historical Publishing Co., 1956.

———— ed., *North Carolina History Told by Contemporaries*. Chapel Hill, N.C.: University of North Carolina Press, 1934.

———— and Powell, William S., *Colonial North Carolina: A History*. New York: Charles Scribner's Sons, 1973.

———— and Newsome, Albert, *North Carolina: The History of a Southern State*. Chapel Hill, N.C.: University of North Carolina Press, 1954.

Martin, François-Xavier, *The History of North Carolina*. New Orleans: Penniman and Co., 1829.

Merrens, Harry Ray, *Colonial North Carolina in the Eighteenth Century*. Chapel Hill, N.C.: University of North Carolina Press, 1964.

Morgan, Lewis H., *Houses and House Life of the American Aborigines*. Chicago: University of Chicago Press, 1965.

Mooney, James. *The Siouan Tribes of the East*. Washington, D.C.: Government Printing Office, 1894.

Moore, Frank, ed., *Diary of the American Revolution, 1775–1781*. New York: Washington Square Press, 1967.

Moore, John W., *History of North Carolina*. Raleigh, N.C.: Alfred Williams and Company, 1880.

Morison, Samuel Eliot, *The European Discovery of America: The Northern Voyages, 500–1600*. New York: Oxford University Press, 1971.

Morris, Richard B., ed., *Encyclopaedia of American History*. New York: Harper and Brothers, 1953.

National Cyclopedia of Biography. New York: James T. White and Company, 1909.

Norman, Charles, *Discoverers of America*. New York: Thomas Y. Crowell Company, 1968.

North Carolina Board of Agriculture, *North Carolina: A General Sketch*. Raleigh, N.C.: P. M. Hale, 1886.

O'Donnell, James H. III, *Southern Indians in the American Revolution*. Knoxville, Tenn.: The University of Tennessee Press, 1973.

Peckham, Howard H., *The War for Independence*. Chicago: University of Chicago Press, 1958.

Phillips, George Lewis, *American Chimney Sweeps: An Historical Account of a Once Important Trade*. Trenton, N.J.: The Past Times Press, 1957.

Pirates of the Spanish Main. New York: American Heritage Publishing Company, 1961.

Quynn, Dorothy Mackay, "Flora MacDonald in History," *North Carolina Historical Review*, Vol. XVIII, No. 3.

Rankin, Hugh F., *North Carolina in the American Revolution*. Raleigh, N.C.: State Department of Archives and History, 1965.

————— *North Carolina Continentals*. Chapel Hill, N.C.: University of North Carolina Press, 1971.

————— *The Pirates of North Carolina*. Raleigh, N.C.: State Department of Archives and History, 1960.

Robinson, Blackwell Pierce, *Battles and Engagements of the American Revolution in North Carolina*. N.p.: Lafayette Chapter of the Daughters of the American Revolution, 1961.

—————, ed., *The North Carolina Guide*. Chapel Hill, N.C.: University of North Carolina Press, 1955.

Ross, Malcolm, *The Cape Fear*. Rivers of America Series. New York: Holt, Rinehart and Winston, 1965.

Russell, Phillips, *North Carolina in the Revolutionary War*. Charlotte, N.C.: Heritage Printers, Inc., 1965.

Spencer, Robert F., Jennings, Jesse D., et al., *The Native Americans*. New York: Harper & Row, 1965.

Terrell, John Upton, *American Indian Almanac*. New York: World Publishing Company, 1971.

Van Every, Dale, *A Company of Heroes*. New York: William Morrow and Company, 1964.

————— *Forth to the Wilderness*. New York: William Morrow and Company, 1961.

Vining, Elizabeth Gray, *Flora, A Biography*. Philadelphia: J. B. Lippincott Company, 1966.

Wheeler, John Hill, *Historical Sketches of North Carolina, from 1684 to 1851*. Baltimore: Regional Publishing Company, 1964.

Whiteford, Andrew Hunter, *North American Indian Arts*. New York: Golden Press, 1970.

Williamson, Hugh, *The History of North Carolina*. Philadelphia: Thomas Dobson, 1812.

Important Dates

1524 Giovanni da Verrazano, a Florentine navigator, explores the coast of North Carolina and claims it for France.

1578 Sir Humphrey Gilbert, half brother of Sir Walter Raleigh, is granted a patent to explore "heathen lands."

1584 Philip Amadas and Arthur Barlowe, sent by Raleigh, explore Roanoke Island and the nearby coast, looking for a suitable place to plant a colony. The land is named Virginia.

1585–86 First English colony is planted in the New World on Roanoke Island. Ralph Lane, Raleigh's lieutenant governor, builds Fort Raleigh, but the colony is later deserted.

1587 John White is sent as governor of another colony on Roanoke Island. His granddaughter, Virginia Dare, is born August 18, the first child of English parents born in the New World.

1590 John White leads a relief expedition back to Roanoke, hoping to find his colony safe. Instead, it has disappeared, leaving only the word "CROTOAN" carved on a tree. Henceforth, it is known as the Lost Colony.

1607 First permanent English colony in the New World is settled at Jamestown, Virginia.

1629 Charles I grants Carolana to Robert Heath.

1629–50 Traders from Virginia explore the region to the south of their own colony, area now known as North Carolina.

1650–60 First settlers gradually move south from Virginia to take up claims in Albemarle.

1662 North Carolina's oldest recorded land grant is made to George Durant.

1663 Charles II grants Carolina to eight Lords Proprietors.

1664 William Drummond of Virginia is appointed first governor of Albemarle. Barbadians make the first settlement on the Cape Fear River, later abandoned.

1665 Charles II extends the boundaries of Carolina northward.

1669 The Fundamental Constitutions of Carolina, drawn up by philosopher John Locke, is issued in England.

1676–80	John Culpeper and George Durant head a revolt against the proprietorial forces of Thomas Miller and Thomas Eastchurch.
1683–89	Governor Seth Sothel tyrannizes over Albemarle until forcibly removed.
1689	Albemarle (North Carolina) is separated administratively from Charleston (South Carolina).
1690	John Gibbs challenges Governor Ludwell to duel "as long as my Eyelids shall wagg."
1700–04	Argument between Quakers and Anglicans over establishment of the Church of England.
1705	Pamticoe, a Huguenot settlement south of Albemarle, is renamed Bath and created the colony's first capital.
1707–10	Thomas Cary, formerly in favor of establishing the church, leads a revolt against the establishment.
1710	Christopher von Graffenried and John Lawson found a colony of German and Swiss settlers and name their town New Bern.
1710	The Tuscarora Indians petition Pennsylvania authorities for permission to move to that colony, out of the reach of aggressive Carolinians. Permission refused.
1711	Lawson and von Graffenried are seized by the Tuscaroras, and Lawson is tortured to death. Indians carry war to the white settlements.
1712–13	Tuscarora Jack Barnwell and later John Moore march to the aid of North Carolina from South Carolina, putting down the Indian revolt.
1712	North Carolina is wholly and finally separated from South Carolina.
1713–18	Edward Teach, the pirate known as Blackbeard, terrorizes the Carolina coast, is protected by North Carolina authorities, and finally is defeated and slain by a party of Virginians and Royal Navy men.
1729	George II purchases the shares of seven of the eight proprietorships. Henceforth, North Carolina is a royal colony.
1730–50	Highland Scots, encouraged by earlier settlers in the Cape Fear valley, migrate to North Carolina. After 1746, when the Highlands are overrun by vengeful British, this trickle swells briefly to a flood.
1735	The first Scotch-Irish arrive by way of Charleston and move inland to the Piedmont.
1741	North Carolina contingents join a British expedition against Cartagena. Only twenty-five out of four hundred are known to have returned.
1747–48	Brunswick and other seaports are raided by Spanish privateers.
1747	The first German settlers arrive, to be joined by seasoned Pennsylvania Dutch.
1753	The first Moravians arrive at Wachovia. George Washington is sent to the Ohio Valley with an ultimatum for the French.
1754	Skirmishes between Washington's force and the French spark the French and Indian War.
1755	Edward Braddock is ambushed and defeated at the Monongahela. A North Carolina force, out scouting at the time, escape the slaughter and evade capture.

1758	Acting on information received from a North Carolina scout, British push on and take Fort Duquesne.
1765–66	Incensed by passage of the Stamp Act, Sons of Liberty force stamp master William Houston to resign, refuse to accept a bribe for their silence, and rescue impounded vessels from naval clutches.
1766	Funds for Tryon's Palace are voted by the assembly, sparking much ill feeling in the impoverished backcountry.
1768–70	The Regulators organize, chiefly in Orange County, and threaten rebellion.
1771	The Regulators are defeated at Alamance Creek by the colonial militia under Governor William Tryon.
1774	Flora MacDonald, husband Allan, and three of their children arrive in North Carolina to build a new life.
1773	The Boston Tea Party excites all the colonies.
1774	North Carolina sends sympathy supplies to beleaguered Boston. The First Provincial Congress meets at New Bern. In Edenton, patriotic ladies express their support for the cause by burning all their tea—the so-called Edenton Tea Party.
1775	Lexington-Concord turns the quarrel into a war, North Carolina's governor flees, and in Mecklenburg County, Patriots proclaim themselves independent of Great Britain—America's first and boldest such declaration.
1776	Highland Scots and other Loyalists march toward Wilmington to spearhead subjugation of the colony. They are met and defeated by Patriots at Moore's Creek Bridge, a battle that gave the South three long years to prepare for war. The Halifax Resolves urge the Continental Congress to declare independence, and in Philadelphia this historic step is taken. The new State of North Carolina gets itself organized.
1778–79	Savannah falls, and war comes to the South.
1780	Charleston is surrendered, Horatio Gates is disastrously defeated at Camden, and Lord Cornwallis enters North Carolina. Meanwhile, guerrilla war breaks out between Patriot and Loyalist partisans. At Kings Mountain the tide begins to turn.
1781	At Cowpens Daniel Morgan defeats Banastre Tarleton, then rejoins Nathanael Greene, the new American commander in the South. At Guilford Courthouse, Cornwallis achieves a Pyrrhic victory over Greene and withdraws his exhausted troops to Virginia. At Yorktown he is forced to surrender, and one by one other southern posts fall to Greene.
1789	The North Carolina constitutional convention ratifies the Constitution, and the former colony becomes the twelfth state.
1790	North Carolina cedes its over-mountain territory to the new United States, later to become the sixteenth state, Tennessee.

Historic Sites

CHARLOTTE

1. Independence Square, at the intersection of Trade and Tryon Streets is the site of the first courthouse, where Colonel Thomas Polk read the Mecklenburg Declaration of Independence. In 1780 Colonel William R. Davie delayed General Cornwallis here in a skirmish. The British occupied the town, and Cornwallis established his headquarters in Colonel Polk's home.
2. The site of Patrick Jack's tavern is at 211 West Trade Street. It was from this tavern that Captain James Jack left to take the news of Mecklenburg's independence to the Continental Congress in Philadelphia.

EDENTON

1. The site of the Edenton Tea Party is marked by a large bronze teapot mounted on a Revolutionary cannon.
2. The Barker House was the home of Penelope Barker who, according to tradition, presided over the Edenton Tea Party.
3. The Chowan County Courthouse was built in 1767 and has been in continuous use ever since. It has been described as "perhaps the finest Georgian courthouse in the South." Upstairs in the Masonic Lodge Room is a chair that was used by George Washington when he was master of the Alexandria, Virginia, lodge.
4. The Cupola House, built about 1712, is of Jacobean design. It is thought to have the first sash windows used in North Carolina. The octagonal cupola was used to sight incoming ships and was illuminated in honor of the king's birthday, public holidays, and other festive occasions.
5. St. Paul's Church, reconstructed in 1948, was first organized in 1701, and the original wooden building was the first church building in North Carolina. In 1711 Reverend John Winston wrote that when the vestry met, "rum was the chief of their business."

ELIZABETH CITY

1. About three miles from Elizabeth City is Enfield Farm, scene of the Culpeper

Rebellion in 1677. When Interim Governor Thomas Miller tried to collect the customs duty, John Culpeper, George Durant, and other antiproprietorial planters seized him, took over the legislature, and for two years ran the government.

2. At Halls Creek, about seventeen miles from Elizabeth City, the assembly of Albemarle was called by William Drummond, first governor of North Carolina, in 1665. This first assembly of settlers in North Carolina is said to have asserted in one of the bylaws that members should "wear shoes, if not stockings" during the session.

ELIZABETHTOWN

1. Elizabethtown, seat of Bladen County, on the western bank of the Cape Fear River, was settled about 1734 by Scots, English, and Irish. In 1773 it was named for Elizabeth (her last name is not known), the sweetheart of Isaac Jones, who gave the land for the town site.
2. The Tory Hole at Broad Street near the center of town is the site of a deep ravine, where retreating Tories took refuge when attacked by Patriots in 1781.

FAYETTEVILLE

1. The northeast corner of Green and Bow Streets is where Flora MacDonald supposedly lived for a few months in 1774–75. Later she went to Mount Pleasant where she stayed with Allen Cameron until her husband, Allan, bought Killigray, his estate on Cheek's Creek in Montgomery County.
2. Cross Creek Cemetery contains the graves of many of the Scots Highlanders.

GREENSBORO

1. In 1771 Guilford County was created from Orange and Rowan Counties and was named for Frederick Lord North, prime minister of England during the Revolution and later earl of Guilford. In 1774, about five miles northwest of present Greensboro, the first courthouse was built, and around it grew up the straggling village of Guilford Courthouse. Here the battle took place on March 15, 1781, between the forces of Charles Earl Cornwallis and those of American Major General Nathanael Greene. The British won a Pyrrhic victory but afterward were forced into an exhausted retreat. After the Revolution the name of the town was changed to Martinville, in honor of the first governor, but when two counties were formed and Martinville was no longer centrally located, a new town was laid out and named Greensboro in honor of General Greene.

HALIFAX

1. As the charming seat of Halifax County, Halifax was the scene of North Carolina's first constitutional convention. In the courthouse, Joseph Hewes, William Hooper, and John Penn were designated delegates to the Continental

Congress. The Halifax Resolves, which were drawn up at this time, were the first official action by any colonial legislature for absolute separation from England and for national independence. In recognition of this fact, the North Carolina flag bears the date April 12, 1776, which is known as Halifax Day and is a state holiday.

HILLSBORO

1. Hillsboro started out as Orange, as did the county. Later it bore the names Corbinton and Childsboro, but in 1766 Governor Tryon named it Hillsboro in honor of the earl of Hillsborough, who was related to Mrs. Tryon. It became a summer capital for the governor, his friends, and wealthy planters from the low-lying coastal plains, who sought refuge there from the heat and mosquitoes. When Cornwallis took Hillsboro before the Battle of Guilford Courthouse, he ordered that the muddy main streets be paved with large cobblestones.

NEW BERN

1. Union Point, at the juncture of the Neuse and Trent rivers, is where Von Graffenried built a government house and fort in 1710 for his town of New Bern. King Taylor of the Tuscarora Indians is said to have lived here at a village called Chattawka, from which Chautauqua, New York, gets its name.
2. The first printing press in North Carolina was operated by James Davis at the corner of East Front and Broad Streets.
3. Tryon's Palace has been authentically restored and is open to the public as a museum. Designed by John Hawks, it combined the governor's residence, assembly hall, council chamber, and public offices. One wing contained servants' quarters and laundry; the other granary and hayloft.

ROANOKE ISLAND

1. Manteo and Wanchese, two small villages, were named for the two Indians who befriended the earliest English settlers.
2. Remains of the original Fort Raleigh, designed by Ralph Lane, governor of the 1585 expedition, have been discovered through archaeological excavations. The fort has been rebuilt on the site, and each year a symphonic drama, *The Lost Colony*—written by Paul Green, a native North Carolinian—is presented at the Waterside Theatre.

SNOW HILL

1. About five miles northwest of Snow Hill is the site of the Tuscarora Indian town of Catechna, where John Lawson and Baron von Graffenried were taken as captives a few days before the Tuscarora Massacre broke out. Lawson was tortured to death, but Von Graffenried was released after several weeks' imprisonment.

WILMINGTON

1. The corner of Front and Market Streets marks the site of the old courthouse, where in 1765 Dr. William Houston, the royal stamp master, was forced to resign. Here, too, three detained merchant ships were released from custody in early 1766 by an anti-Stamp Act mob.
2. The Cornwallis House at the southwest corner of Market and Third Streets is said to have been the headquarters of the English general while he was in possession of the city in April, 1781. Original floor boards show marks supposedly made by British muskets. The basement was used as a military prison.
3. The original St. James' Episcopal Church was built in 1751 and was presented with a painting of Christ, "Ecce Homo," which was taken from a Spanish pirate ship when it attacked the town of Brunswick in 1748.
4. Town Creek, about nine miles from Wilmington, is the site of the first settlement on the Cape Fear River in 1660, by a party of New Englanders. In 1661 and 1663 exploring parties from Barbadoes paved the way for a settlement in 1664 which Barbadians called Charles Town. It was abandoned in 1667.
5. Old Brunswick, south of Wilmington, was founded by Maurice Moore, father of Judge Maurice and General James Moore, Revolutionary Patriots. In 1729, when New Hanover County was established, Brunswick became the county seat, but Wilmington quickly outgrew it as a trade center, and in 1740 all governmental offices were moved there.

WINSTON-SALEM

1. Old Salem (which means "peace") was founded in 1766 by a group of Moravians from the original settlement of Bethabara. When the site was selected, twelve men were sent to cut logs for the first house. Lots were not sold but were leased for one year, subject to renewal so long as the tenant was satisfactory to the community. The town is now in the process of being restored.

Index